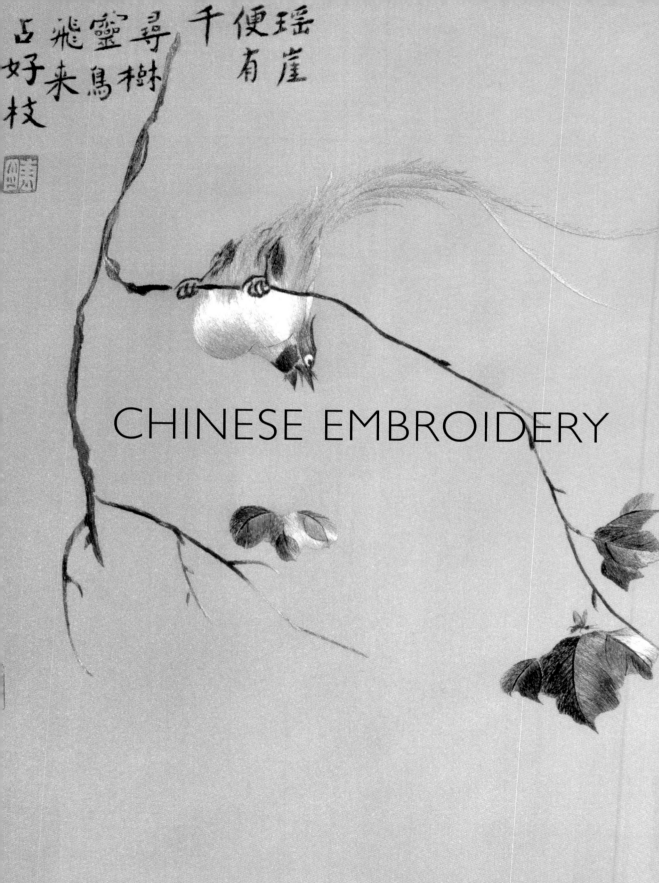

CHINESE EMBROIDERY
An Illustrated Stitch Guide

Shao Xiaocheng

Over 40 Exquisite Projects

Better Link Press

On page 1
FIG. 1   *Chinese Parasol and Paradise Flycatcher* by Shao Xiaocheng
Gu-Style Embroidery (*Gu Xiu*)
The paradise flycatcher represents longevity and the Chinese parasol is a spirited tree which stands good wishes. Therefore, this embroidered article symbolizes happiness and auspiciousness. In the embroidered article, a paradise flycatcher is chirping on the tree-branch while a humming bee rests on a leaf in the right lower corner, presenting a scene of dynamism and quietness. The silk color of this embroidered article is exquisite since strands were divided for application. For example, white colors of five different grades were used in embroidering the paradise flycatcher. As a result, needlework free from restraint can be displayed via the technique of painting, making the embroidery look elegant, tender, and soft.

It was selected to take part in the Exhibition of Arts and Crafts, which celebrated the 60th anniversary of the founding of the PRC by the National Art Museum of China in 2009, the Exhibition of Contemporary High-Quality Embroidery Art of the Chinese Museum of Women and Children in 2011, and the Biennial of Arts and Crafts of National Museum of China in 2012.

On page 2
FIG. 2   *The Beauty—Xishi*
A success should be made of embroidering five facial organs when a human figure is embroidered. The key is in the eyes since eye expression reveals the soul of the figure. Xishi is a famous beauty in Chinese history. While looking down, her face is reflected in the lake's water. Her implicit eye expression adds to her appeal.

This book is edited and designed by the Editorial Committee of *Cultural China* series.

Text by Shao Xiaocheng
Works by Shao Xiaocheng, Xiao Yao
Photographs by Xiao Lin
Translation by Cao Jianxin
Cover Design by Wang Wei
Interior Design by Li Jing (Yuan Yinchang Design Studio)

Copy Editor: Susan Luu Xiang
Editors: Yang Xiaohe, Wu Yuezhou
Editorial Director: Zhang Yicong

Senior Consultants: Sun Yong, Wu Ying, Yang Xinci
Managing Director and Publisher: Wang Youbu

ISBN: 978-1-60220-015-9

Address any comments about *Chinese Embroidery: An Illustrated Stitch Guide* to:

Better Link Press
99 Park Ave
New York, NY 10016
USA

or

Shanghai Press and Publishing Development Company
F 7 Donghu Road, Shanghai, China (200031)
Email: comments_betterlinkpress@hotmail.com

Printed in China by Shenzhen Donnelley Printing Co., Ltd.

3   5   7   9   10   8   6   4   2

CONTENTS

FIG. 3 *A Colourful Flower Basket (Part)*
Colorful threads are used as auxiliary threads in patterns of gold thread couching stitch since they cannot only fix gold threads but also add further excellence to the embroidery. First of all, gold and silver threads can present rich changes only by means of the color of the tacking threads. Besides, at places needed, the use of colorful threads can produce unexpected desirable effects. In this picture, the embroiderer applied bright orange-red threads on the silver day lily, making it lively.

CHAPTER FOUR
Embroidery Projects for Daily Use *89*

CONTENTS

PREFACE

I am fond of dividing embroidery into several stages.

From seven to nine years of age, I lived in a small town in the south of the Yangtze River in China, a town in which all households were engaged in embroidery. I played with my friends in the neighborhood, but they always had a lot to embroider and not enough time for me. So I helped them with their embroidery in order to play with them after the work was done. I had been to almost all my friends' homes doing embroidery, the ones who lived on the same street as me. At that time, the embroidery of each household was different from one another, i.e. Western lace embroidery, embroidery on woolen sweaters, net-patterned embroidery on children's clothes, and of course, Chinese embroidery. More often than not, children would start to embroider after watching each other for a short while, as if they were born to do it. Perhaps I already enjoyed embroidering at that time, hence repeatedly doing it in spite of myself and became interested in it just like playing games.

In high school, I took a fancy to literature and painting. In those famous works of literature and poetry, I often found such description related to embroidery as "embroidery frame and stand," "embroidery girl," "fine embroidery," "embroidered belvedere," and "embroidered painting" as well as embroidered garments worn by the rich and officials. These descriptions blessed me with a sense for unique beauty. Therefore, I often incorporated patterns of embroidery into paintings of beautiful girls, i.e. incorporate patterns of embroidery from the Tang and Ming dynasties to the garments of beautiful girls in the paintings of those periods. Of course, it wouldn't do by resorting to imagination when incorporating these patterns of embroidery to garments through painting. I would look it up in history books to get to know the history, customs, habits, garment

FIG. 4 *Boating at Leisure* by Shao Xiaocheng
Shandong Embroidery
This was completed by imitating the technique of Shandong Embroidery (*lu xiu*) in the Ming style. Being faithful to the craftsmanship of four hundred years ago, it presents embroidered hill-peaks, water ripples, and rocks by means of simple couching stitch and feathering technique with several strands of threads on a par with each other. Silk threads were used to embroider the whole piece, having perfectly, with softness in hardness, brought about the leisure of a recluse fishing on the boat amidst hills and the river together with the sceneries of Mother Nature. The temperament of the expansive picture is harmoniously integrated with fairly rough and unrestrained needlework, fully revealing the style and features of Shandong Embroidery marked by the roughness, simplicity, robustness, and masculine gender of Shandong Embroidery, as well as representing the artistic mien of embroidery in northern China in the Ming Dynasty.

Shandong Embroidery is almost lost. The author is embroidering it for preservation since it is of fairly great value for research and protection.

(The image on page 3 is the detailed part of the image on the facing page.)

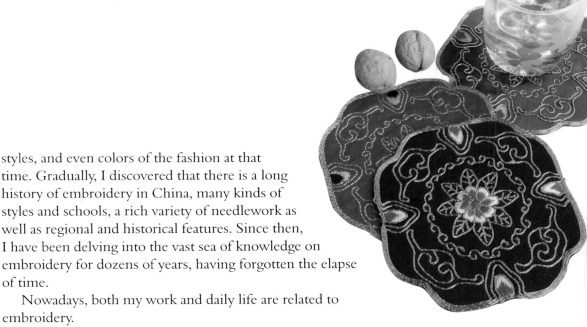

styles, and even colors of the fashion at that time. Gradually, I discovered that there is a long history of embroidery in China, many kinds of styles and schools, a rich variety of needlework as well as regional and historical features. Since then, I have been delving into the vast sea of knowledge on embroidery for dozens of years, having forgotten the elapse of time.

Nowadays, both my work and daily life are related to embroidery.

"Stand" is related to embroidery—I teach students embroidery, do research on embroidery, take part in activities for the exchange of ideas on embroidery, and hold embroidery exhibitions.

"Sit" is related to embroidery—I engage in creating embroidery works, studying the history of embroidery, writing books and articles on embroidery, and appraise and repair of ancient embroidery.

"Travel" is related to embroidery—I make investigation into the culture of embroidery among common folks and probe into and protect embroidery craftsmanship.

"Hate" is related to embroidery—I am willingly and absolutely obsessed with the huge glamor of embroidery all my life.

"Love" is related to embroidery—It gives me boundless happiness, cordiality, and joy.

Its gentle elegance is like murmuring spring water with a sweet taste and refreshing spring breeze that can be enjoyed by an individual and shared by all. Embroidery is an important part that is inseparable from my life.

FIG. 5　*Morning Glory* by Shao Xiaocheng

By means of needlework, this embroidered article demonstrates the artistic features of brushwork and ink application of Chinese paintings marked by burnt black, moisture, heaviness, lightness, thickness and stainlessness. Morning glory blossoms before dawn represents diligence. The embroidered morning glory appears vigorous, almost detaching itself from the picture.

In 1995, it won the Award of Excellence at the 4th World Conference on Women and took part in a world tour. In 2000, it was brought into *Contemporary High-Quality Arts and Crafts of China* of Jiangsu Fine-Art Publishing House and later borrowed by the Jiangsu Aitao Hall of High-Quality Artworks for exhibition. Now, it is preserved in the Beijing Shao Xiaocheng Embroidery Research Institute.

INTRODUCTION

The beginning, development, and evolution of Chinese embroidery do not seek for grand brilliance, but its beauty and vibrancy enjoy a long history. It is vividly represented in the spiritual and daily lives of hundreds and thousands of people, reflecting their pursuit for beauty and love for life. The different styles of embroidery techniques handed down from generation to generation are like sweet spring water, keeping the gentleness of human nature from going dry. A partial examination of Chinese embroidery will be enough to enable you to form an understanding of it. Whether you enjoy turning out embroidery with needlework at your leisure or endeavor to create beautiful designs with your fingertips, some background knowledge is always helpful.

Chinese embroidery has a long history. All the dynasties had their own representations of embroidery that reflected the craftsmanship, social life, spirit, and culture of those historic periods, which cherished the splendid several thousand years' history of China. So much of the emotion and wisdom of the embroiderers are embodied in the form, patterns, needlework, structuring, and the selection of thread texture, color, and material of each piece of embroidery. Their meticulous design from conception to application reveals a very high artistic value.

However, how does one appreciate a piece of nice embroidery? Each exquisite piece of embroidery can be appreciated roughly from several aspects:

Evenness. Threads appear neat without being too sparse, thick, and tight.

Flatness. Needlework is marked by evenness, clear outlines, and smooth and neat threads without showing the fabric.

Harmony. Colors are interesting and complement each other.

Light. The brightness of a lustrous color fabric surface is enhanced through skillful needlework and strict craftsmanship.

FIG. 6 *Tara* by Shao Xiaocheng
Suzhou Embroidery
Tara stands for eliminating disasters, increasing happiness, prolonging life, and developing wisdom. This embroidered article was produced through over ten kinds of needlework in five and half months by taking archaistic real silk as high-grade fabrics. Tara sitting at the center is made serene, dignified, pretty, merciful, and auspicious through embroidery, revealing the solemnity and seriousness of religion as well as the grand beauty of Buddhist painting.

It is extremely difficult to embroider through imitating the painting of religious themes. Only by possessing high techniques of embroidery and understanding Buddhism can embroiderers endow embroidered articles with profound connotation.

Smoothness. Vivid patterns, practical arrangement of thread directions and curves that are free from stiffness.

Fineness. Finely arrayed threads without any trace of stitches, as if the embroidery is painted onto the fabric surface.

Ingenuity. A variety of needlework is combined, while embroidering techniques are rich, varying, and natural, showing the meticulousness of the embroiderer. Each detail of craftsmanship can be incorporated perfectly with patterns.

Meticulousness. No painting-manuscript is seen on the fabric, no color is applied, and no background color can be referred to, except outlines. The embroidery is completed purely with the help of needle and threads. Though not the painting, the embroidery is nicer than the painting, possessing very talented artistic craftsmanship.

Cleanness. Free from color-loss, color-fading, dirt, and damage.

Uniqueness. With traditional features of excellent embroidery schools, they have patterns different from those sold in the market. Special threads are applied for creation plus complex craftsmanship and process, hence displaying a unique style.

Daily use embroidery is supposed to be attractive, practical, solid, and washable. Embroidery for appreciation, apart from being beautiful due to exquisite craftsmanship, should also be infused with the artistic appeal of Chinese and Western paintings, marked either by the appreciation of embroidery, or by the elegant style of noted painters.

Chinese embroidery is characterized by diversity, various schools, plentiful needlework, and evolving styles. Unlike other kinds of embroidery, it is not easy to turn out fixed illustrations of needlework, write books concerned, and popularize it among readers in terms of Chinese embroidery. Therefore, while writing this book, I endeavored to express, with simple illustrated examples, most of the needlework of Chinese embroidery. This includes the needlework that can be maneuvered by the independent needlework and combined ones derived from a variety of needlework. This way, readers can understand and experience through factual examples and perceive methods concerned in the course of trying to embroider in person, in addition to comprehending by analogy and stimulating

FIG. 7 *Kittens* by Shao Xiaocheng
Suzhou Embroidery
Those kittens of Chinese Suzhou Embroidery are famous for its meticulous needlework and vivid image. Very often, nearly ten stitches were applied, including split stitch, shaded satin stitch, slanted satin stitch, etc. Requirements were also made for the application of silk threads, i.e., according to the features of kittens, the texture of dense, fine, soft and fluffy cat hair should be brought about. Two threads and one-and-half threads of different layers and colors were applied to reach the effect of harmonious color, flexible turning, natural hair, and vivid image.

the imagination and creation of the individual. In this way, it will not be difficult to produce ideal embroidery.

Examples of needlework techniques are arranged according to the evolution of embroidery, in order to make it convenient for readers to get to know the style of different schools, as well as their development in each stage and the chronological order of those kinds of embroidery along with their history. This way, readers can learn techniques of embroidery and also increase their knowledge of its history. Meanwhile, there are comments of appreciation and analysis of high-quality Chinese embroidery and introduction to the basic knowledge of embroidery collection. I believe readers can enjoy reading it, experiencing it, and learning from it. This is my sincere wish in writing this book for you all.

CHAPTER ONE
A BRIEF HISTORY OF CHINESE EMBROIDERY

Since its birth in China, embroidery as an ancient craftsmanship known to all, has always been beautifying and serving life over the past several thousand years, leaving brilliant and untold excellence for people generation after generation. Based on the rich accumulation of traditional embroidery, contemporary embroidery is also successfully developing in China.

1. Origin—in Remote Antiquity

It is very difficult for us to ascertain the time and place for the birth of embroidery in Chinese antiquity. However, there is no doubt that it originated from the era when human textile and sewing were born. The earliest embroidery started from tattooing, which was later turned into handcraftsmanship applied to garment decoration in close combination with practical and attractive decoration in daily life. It was the beginning of the change from backward facial tattooing to civilization and progress of human beings. A bone needle unearthed from the Upper Cave Man Site in Zhoukoudian in Beijing dates back 8,000 years. It is 8.2 centimeters long, with the widest part being 0.33 centimeters in diameter. So far, it is the earliest sewing tool known in the world (FIG. 9). One can imagine that when the processing of needles, threads, and fabrics was available, it was natural for the emergence of products for sewing and embroidery.

Prior to the emergence of cotton and linen fabrics, our predecessors in antiquity resorted to leather tanning for clothes. They brought about patterns on leather clothes by using bone needles to sew leather stripes or plant fibers, which was closer to the habit of tattooing. Before accurate excavated objects can be used as evidence, we can deduce that prior to the emergence of fabric, application of embroidery onto leather may be more frequently seen. A leather belt embroidered with silk that was unearthed from Tianxingguan Tomb in Hubei Province in 1978 may serve as evidence of this deduction. It is 40 centimeters long and 7 centimeters wide. The leather is covered with a layer of silk tabby embroidered with brown and dark yellow silk-threaded circling hornless dragon (*chi*) patterns. The top and the bottom are embroidered with horizontal S-shaped patterns (FIG.10).

FIG. 8   Embroidery in the imitation of the phoenix patterns of the Pre-Qin period

FIG. 9   A sketch map of the bone needle as used by the Upper Cave Man at Zhoukoudian in Beijing

FIG. 10   A silk embroidered belt of the Warring States Period preserved in Jingzhou Museum, Hubei Province

2. Early Emergence—the Western Zhou Period (1046–771 BC)

Based on present archaeological excavations, the immature dyeing techniques at the time did not make it possible for color to be applied to threads before stitching. Instead, color was applied after the embroidered patterns were finished. Let's take a look at the marks of silk fabric with patterns embroidered in chain stitch from the Western Zhou Period that was found in the mud in the Tomb of Yubo in Baoji, Shaanxi Province in 1974. With this kind of embroidery, patterns were first outlined by yellow silk threads on the dyed silk fabric and then big patches of color were smeared and dyed on the embroidered patterns, including such colors as red (natural cinnabar) and yellow (realgar), etc. This was the feature of embroidery in its early period of development (FIG.11).

Fabrics used for embroidery in this period did not have close-knit fibers. Therefore, patterns embroidered were sparser than those in the following generation. It was even more evident if the fabrics were cotton, linen, and wool. For instance, in 1978, a piece of woolen embroidery from the Western Zhou Period unearthed from the Ancient Cemetery Area in Wubao, Xinjiang Uygur Autonomous Region is marked by a reddish brown wool with plain woven fabrics structured with the same warp and weft. Gorgeous geometric patterns in small triangles were embroidered with running stitch by white wool threads as well as threads dyed in yellow, blue, and pale green. When unearthed, they were seen over the body of a dead female. So far, it is the earliest embroidered object (FIG.12).

FIG. 11   Traces of chain stitch on a silt of the Western Zhou Dynasty preserved in Baoji Museum, Shaanxi Province

FIG. 12   Woolen embroidery with running stitch of the Western Zhou Dynasty preserved in the Museum of Xinjiang Uygur Autonomous Region

3. Taking Form—the Spring and Autumn Period, the Warring States Period, the Qin and the Han Periods (770 BC–220 AD)

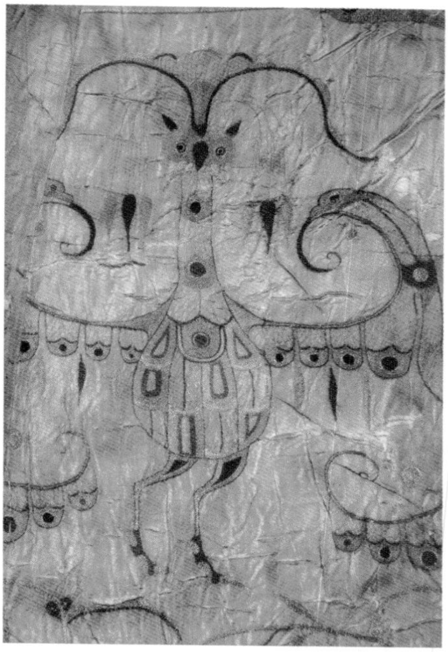

During the Spring and Autumn Period and the Warring States Period (770–221 BC), embroidery was brought about by single chain stitch needlework. The most representative was a batch of embroidery in the middle and late stage of the Warring States Period (475–221 BC) that was unearthed from Chu State Tombs of Jiangling County, Hubei Province. Though buried underground for over 2,000 years, they still appear gorgeous with exquisite patterns and vivid styles. They are well preserved in big numbers featured by delicate and mature skills of embroidery. There are mostly over ten kinds of colors, i.e. brown, reddish brown, dark brown, eosin, vermilion, orange-red, golden yellow, earthen yellow, yellowish-green, dark green, blue, and grey, etc. Each pattern is combined with three to five kinds of colors that are mainly in warm hues in sharp contrast. Patterns are chiefly marked by dragons, phoenixes, tigers, and flowers. These different patterns look beautiful, neat, unrestrained, vivid, and regularly laid out with changes in symmetrical distribution and interaction in smoothness (FIG. 13).

The development of embroidery benefited from the unification of different states in China in the Qin Period and the Han Period (221 BC–220 AD) when the system of conferment was replaced by the system of centralism. Economic and cultural exchanges and integration became increasingly extensive. Social and agricultural production as well as handicraft production became increasingly prosperous. The textile industry developed rapidly, leading to the emergence of professional embroiderers. Apart from silk embroidery, embroidery on woolen products is also often seen among embroidered articles unearthed in north-west China. Motifs of embroidered patterns became richer. In addition to mature chain stitch, short running stitch, blanket stitch and bead work also began to appear. They were new

FIG. 13　Embroidery of Phoenix Patterns Warring States Period

The most representative embroidery in ancient China was none other than chain stitch between the Warring States Period and the Han Dynasty. Despite its mono-needlework and unchanged craftsmanship, its needlework was neat and unrestrained, its patterns were spirited and regularly laid out with changes in symmetric distribution and interaction amidst smoothness. Such features can be found in many embroidered articles unearthed in the same period.

Phoenix was regarded as a mythological bird in remote antiquity in China. Therefore, it was frequently seen on embroidered patterns at that time. Its flowing posture is varied, full of rhythm as well as miraculous and illusive appeal, revealing the appeal of aesthetics and the style of romanticism of the culture of the Chu state in the Warring States Period. For instance, the phoenix in this embroidered article is marked by a high crown, expansive wings, lowering head at one end of the wing, and slightly curved feet, seemingly flying in the air or coming back from the fairyland in romantic conception and gorgeous colors. The entire article was produced with chain stitch, meticulous, and proficient needlework without any trace of stiffness, showing superb embroidery needlework of folk artists more than 2,000 years ago.

embroidery technique used to try to combine patterns. The development of mineral dyestuff and application of plant dyestuff further expanded the color spectrum of threads for embroidery.

Embroidery is of practical use, but it is not only confined to the garment since it has begun to be associated with daily decorative articles, such as sachets, gloves, pillow-towels, needle-thread containers, parcels with lace trimmings, brocade robes, knee-pads, suspenders, face powder bags (FIG. 14), mirror bags, vamps, ribbons, and embroidered trousers, etc. As an important turning point in the history of embroidery, it laid the foundation for the enhancement of the artistry of embroidery in the following generations. What deserves to be stressed is that representative patterns of embroidery appeared in the Qin Period and the Han Period, i.e. embroidery with swallow motif and embroidery with auspicious cloud motif. As terms of embroidery, the two patterns were seen in literature at that time, showing that the popularity and professionalism of embroidery were quite well-grounded.

4. Maturity—the Southern and Northern Dynasties, the Sui Dynasty, and the Tang Dynasty (420–907)

What about embroidery in the Southern and Northern Dynasties? The answer is in the colorful decorative embroideries on the supporters of Buddha statues that were discovered in the Dunhuang Mogao Grottos in Gansu Province in the 1960s (FIG. 15). Buddhism was popular in the Southern and Northern Dynasties. Naturally, more religious objects were decorated by the craftsmanship of embroidery. Although the same chain stitch needlework was applied to some articles of embroidery in the Northern Wei Dynasty (386–534), the rise, rhythm, and exquisiteness in animal-shaped patterns were still pervasive. The content of these patterns were added with elements of decoration and artistic paintings. Depiction of human figures in Buddhist embroidery was accurate in detail, making all creatures in Mother Nature vivid, including birds, dragons, flowers, grass, trees, and fruits. The design of craftsmanship was exceptionally artistic just like a picture with emotion and sceneries, showing that the artists

FIG. 15 Colorful Embroidery of Supporters of Buddha Statues Southern and Northern Dynasties
Supporters are referred to as patrons in Buddhist activities. Anyone who invests in building Buddhist grottos and offers sacrifice to Buddha statues can have his image painted or embroidered under Buddha statues as a benefactor. This embroidered article is preserved in Dunhuang Research Institute, Gansu Province.

FIG. 16 A remaining piece of bead work embroidery in the Tang Dynasty preserved in the Administration Office of Cultural Relics, Kazakh Autonomous Prefecture, Xinjiang Uygur Autonomous Region

FIG. 17 Mandarin Ducks and Peonies (Detail)
Embroidery on Dark Yellow Twill Damask
Tang Dynasty
Discovered in the Thousand Buddha Caves of Dunhuang, embroidery on this plain color twill damask with indistinct flowers of the Tang Dynasty is marked by bright colors, a variety of needlework, and novel patterns. Entwining peony was turned out by gold thread couching stitch to reinforce the sense of stereoscope. Vivid and lovely little birds flying across flowers were brought about by gold thread couching stitch for patterns. Flowers and leaves were embroidered in green of different grades by running stitch. Outlines of leaf-stems and leaves were all decorated by simple couching stitch, hence giving prominence to patterns, both decorative and realistic.

In embroidered works of flower patterns from the Tang Dynasty, flower postures and structure of branches and leaves were mostly rather stiff, lacking the contrast between yin and yang. However, this embroidered article is featured by rich layers of color-matching on flowers, color-change of different grades on leaves, elegant curved branches, gorgeous tints, and changeable needlework, hence making itself one of the highest quality among all embroidered articles from the Tang Dynasty.

already had the innovative awareness of changing embroidery for practical use to embroidery for appreciation.

The prosperity of the Sui Dynasty and the Tang Dynasty ushered in the continuous development of Chinese embroidery. Extensive emergence of religious embroidery marked by embroidered scriptures and embroidered Buddhist paintings stimulated the vigorous progress of embroidery craftsmanship. In this period, chain stitch needlework of embroidery lost its leading position. From the embroidered articles of the Tang Dynasty, we have found bead work (FIG. 16), straight satin stitch, gold thread couching stitch, etc. Thus, there was more expression in embroidery in the Tang Dynasty (FIG. 17). Embroidered garments and bags and *kasaya* (FIG. 18) of the Tang Dynasty collected in British Museum are witness to gorgeous and novel needlework of the Tang embroidery. Petals on the Tang *kasaya* were embroidered with a feathering-

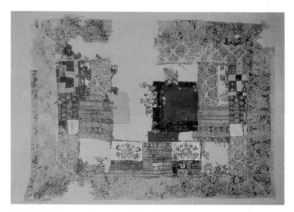

FIG. 18 A *kasaya* from the Tang Dynasty unearthed in Thousand Buddha Caves of Dunhuang, now preserved in the British Museum

like effect, making the picture more vivid, three-dimensional, elegant, and eye-catching while expanding the use of threads. Having completely changed the forms and modes in patterns prior to the Tang Dynasty, this laid the foundation for the development of realism of embroidery in the Song Dynasty.

5. The Prime Period—the Song Dynasty (960–1279)

The Song Dynasty was the cradle for the birth of artistic embroidery, exerting a far-reaching influence on the development of Chinese embroidery. Its art is still highly respected (FIGS. 19, 20). Artistic embroidery benefited from the promotion of paintings in the Song Dynasty in which the royal court witnessed a batch of outstanding painters. Their art, if perceived according to the view in contemporary times, is still glorious and incomparable in terms of achievements. In addition, the royal family of the Song Dynasty exerted unified management over the production of embroidery, having set up Directorate for Imperial Manufactories, Crafts Institute, Embroidery Office, Ornaments Office, Silk Brocade Workshop, and Palace Weaving and Dyeing Office, providing favorable objective conditions for the maturity of artistic embroidery. Particularly under the reign of Emperor Zhao Ji in the Song Dynasty (1100–1126), an Embroidered Painting Specialty was established in Imperial Academy of Painting. Embroiderers of this

FIG. 19 *Chrysanthemum*
Song Dynasty
This embroidered article is characterized by chrysanthemums in full blossom, flying butterflies, dragon flies, and bees. Colorful thread-matching is gorgeous and elegant, showing exquisite craftsmanship of embroidery in the Song Dynasty. It is now preserved in the Palace Museum, Taipei.

FIG. 20 *Majestic Eagle*
Song Dynasty
Its high-rising head, firm chests, and forceful claws were well embroidered. Despite the fall-off of lots of threads due to a long period of time, the eagle still maintains its majesty. This is obviously closely associated with superb techniques of the embroiderer. In spite of extremely fine strands divided and exquisite needlework for feathers, the eagle looks fierce and firm all the same. There were more kinds of innovative needlework for application, showing that embroidery in the Song Dynasty reached art height of immense realism.

The eagle was a painting theme favored by scholars in their painting in the Song Dynasty. Versatile Zhao Ji, Emperor Huizong of the Song Dynasty, was not only good at handwriting, but also at painting flowers, bamboos, feathers, and flowers in water-ink. His *Imperial Eagle* was detailed and unrestrained in depiction, fully revealing its majesty and fierceness without any roughness and wildness. This embroidered article bears strong resemblance to the spirit of Zhao Ji's *Imperial Eagle*. People cannot help applauding such appeal of embroidery from the Song Dynasty.

FIG. 21   *White Eagle*
Song Dynasty
The eagle was used as part of the garment of warriors in the Tang Dynasty and often compared to a hero. It was quite popular in the Song Dynasty, Liao Dynasty, Jin Dynasty, and Yuan Dynasty. This embroidered article is now preserved in the Palace Museum, Taipei.

FIG. 22   *Hibiscus and Crab*
Song Dynasty
This embroidered article was imitation of a painting by Huang Quan (?–965), who was a painter in the imperial court of the Western Shu Dynasty. Most of his paintings were associated with unique birds and famous flowers in the imperial court, showing meticulousness, splendidness, wealth, and nobility. *Hibiscus and Crab* is now preserved in the Palace Museum, Taipei.

specialty all used works of academy painters to create embroidery. Since the art of calligraphy and painting in the Song Dynasty provided plentiful painting-sketches for embroidery, artistic embroidery developed rapidly. An unprecedentedly high starting point gave rise to the vigorous development of embroidery art in the Song Dynasty. A number of artistic embroidery in the Song Dynasty all took the brushwork, lines, colors, and spiritual appeal of the Song paintings as standards of art, even over striding paintings. They brought the Song embroidery to the peak of amazing vividness and formed embroidery for appreciation independent of previous kinds, such as *Plum-Flower, Bamboo and Parrot*, *White Eagle* (FIG. 21), *Riding Crane to Yaotai*, *Okra and Butterflies*, and *Hibiscus and Crab* (FIG. 22).

After that, artistic embroidery advanced ahead as a late-comer and progressed together with embroidery for practical use with a long history, greatly expanding the space for the survival and development of embroidery, leading the style of embroidery creation by many noted embroiderers and the growth of various schools of embroidery, and enabling the art of Chinese embroidery to enter a new period.

6. Carrying Forward the Cause and Forging Ahead into Future—the Yuan Dynasty and the Ming Dynasty (1271–1644)

As discovered in the many years of embroidery research of the Yuan Dynasty, there was a kind of unique fishing-net embroidery which is rarely seen and known in the following generations. It is evidence of dividing history into dynastic periods for appraising and appreciating ancient embroidery, having a far-reaching significance on studying and perceiving embroidery in the Yuan Dynasty (FIG. 23).

FIG. 23 An Embroidered Pad of Flower Patterns Yuan Dynasty
Needlework for the lotus flowers, lotus leaves, white geese, and butterflies on the surface is ordinary, except that the triangle decorative fringes around are quite special. This kind of needlework is similar to fishing-net stitch. Therefore, it is called fishing-net embroidery. This embroidered article is now preserved in the Museum of Inner Mongolian Autonomous Region.

There were no schools of embroidery to speak of in the Ming Dynasty, only with Gu-Style Embroidery (*gu xiu*) and Shandong Embroidery (*lu xiu*) as representatives.

Shandong Embroidery inherited relatively rough and uninhibited features of embroidery for appreciation in the Yuan Dynasty and used double-ply threads. In most cases, a whole thread was used for embroidery. The layout was natural and vivid thanks to direct application of bright colors and the characteristics of freedom and dignity, hence becoming the best among all kinds of embroidery in northern China. Long-standing and classic works of Shandong Embroidery are none other than *Hibiscus and Two Ducks* and *Mandarin Ducks amidst the Lotus Pond*, etc.

Gu-Style Embroidery inherited the delicate application of silk embodied in the embroidered calligraphy and paintings of Song Dynasty embroidery, marked by the application of soft and tender colors as well as extremely thin threads through thread division. Enjoying much pursuit, appreciation, and admiration of scholars and men of letters, Gu-Style Embroidery influenced the style of embroidery in southern China.

The founder of Gu-Style Embroidery was Miao Ruiyun, one of the womenfolk of the Gu family. *Withered Trees, Bamboos, and Rocks* is the only real object left behind as an evidence of her embroidery art (FIG. 24).

Gu-Style Embroidery in early years was basically for family collection or given as gifts. Female embroiderers in the Gu family strive for appreciation, or it could be further viewed as pursuit of upper-class women for art attainment. In terms of embroidery art among female embroiderers in the Gu family, the most representative embroiderer was none other than Han Ximeng, grand daughter-in-law of Gu Mingshi. All her embroidered landscape, human figures, flowers, and birds were "exclusively exquisite."

From the very beginning, Gu-Style Embroidery endeavored to imperceptibly take the lead in the concept of creation for artistic embroidery. As a result, folk embroidery started to truly form new channels for developing artistic embroidery, bringing new prospects of growth to folk embroidery lasting for over 1,000 years (FIG. 25).

7. A Hundred Flowers in Blossom—the Qing Dynasty (1644–1911)

In the Qing Dynasty, embroidery was extensively distributed in China with a wide variety in great numbers and different styles. Moreover, official institutions got involved in management, hence leading to the maturity and development of artistic embroidery for appreciation, i.e. four major schools of embroidery gradually took shape.

Suzhou in Jiangsu Province was the center of embroidery from the middle and late Qing Dynasty. The embroidery that came from that region was known as Suzhou Embroidery (*su xiu*). Sichuan Embroidery (*shu xiu*) was produced in Chengdu in Sichuan Province. Hunan Embroidery (*xiang xiu*) was created in Changsha in Hunan Province. Guangzhou Embroidery (*guang xiu*) came from Guangzhou in Guangdong Province. Chaozhou Embroidery (*chao xiu*) was from Chaozhou. Guangzhou Embroidery and Chaozhou

FIG. 24 *Withered Trees, Bamboos, and Rocks*
Ming Dynasty
Gu-Style Embroidery
Miao Ruiyun, a concubine of the Gu family in the Luxiang Garden, was already good at embroidery of the Song Dynasty when she was a girl. Inheriting the excellent tradition of embroidery of the Song Dynasty, she made innovation in needlework application, color-matching, and material selection. At that time, there was already the saying that "Gu-Style Embroidery started from Miao Ruiyun in Shanghai." This embroidered article is now preserved in the Shanghai Museum.

FIG. 25 *A Pheasant and a White Rabbit*
It is an embroidered work of the Ming Dynasty preserved in the Suzhou Embroidery Research Institute.

FIG. 26 Female Figure by Shao Xiaocheng
Simulation Embroidery

Simulation embroidery was a new technique created by Shen Shou, an artist of Suzhou Embroidery in the late Qing Dynasty. She integrated the strong points of Western fine arts with traditional Chinese needlework to express the yin and yang layers as well as shading perspectives of photography. Her innovation became a milestone in the circle of Suzhou Embroidery in the late Qing Dynasty.

This portrait was embroidered by the author through simulation embroidery. A variety of traditional Chinese needlework and embroidery technique were combined and merged with Western art of light effects. Only outlines and patchy lines are seen on the fabric, without any base of painting and color, hence appropriately revealing the youthfulness, pure beauty, plumpness, and quietness of a young girl as well as very proficiently applying the technique of simulation embroidery. This embroidered article is preserved by an individual in Taiwan.

FIG. 27 *Dragon* by Shen Shou (1874–1921)
Late Qing Dynasty

Shen Shou was first known as Yunzhi. In 1904, she embroidered eight works including a Buddha portrait and contributed them to the imperial court of the Qing Dynasty to celebrate the birthday of Empress Dowager Cixi to her great satisfaction. Cixi conferred a Chinese first name *shou* (longevity) on her. Later, she was sent by the Qing government to go to Japan for the exchange and research of embroidery and painting. After returning to China, she created simulation embroidery, having initiated a new style in the history of contemporary embroidery in China. This embroidered article is now preserved in the Suzhou Museum.

Embroidery were both called Guangdong Embroidery (*yue xiu*). In fact, it was not an accident that they became popular.

Let's first take a look at Suzhou Embroidery, which is one of the four famous embroidery schools with a two-thousand-year history. As the earliest real object of Suzhou Embroidery, an embroidered coffin poll was unearthed in 1981 in Gaoyou, Jiangsu Province, from the tomb of Madame Liu, wife of Liu Xu, Guangling King from the Western Han Dynasty (about 135 BC–87 AD). This cover was embroidered by means of chain stitch needlework, presenting vivid and smooth flowing clouds, birds, animals, flowers, grass, and curved tree-branches. In the 1950s, remaining parts of embroidered Buddhist scriptures were also unearthed from under the pagoda of Yunyan Temple (built in 961) in Huqiu, Suzhou. In Suzhou in the Song Dynasty, there were such workshops of embroidery as Court-Dress Lane (*gunxiu fang*), Brocade Embroidery Lane (*jinxiu fang*), Embroidered Clothes Lane (*xiuyi fang*), Embroidered Flower Lane (*xiuhua nong*), and Embroidery Thread Lane (*xiuxian xiang*), etc. where embroidery works were produced. In the Ming Dynasty, Suzhou became the center of the silk industry marked by "Silkworm-breeding in every household and embroidery in every family," basically forming a style of meticulousness, elegance, and cleanness. In the Qing Dynasty, a variety of Suzhou Embroidery and lots of embroidery shops emerged. In Suzhou alone, there were over 150 embroidery shops with more than 40,000 embroiderers (FIGS. 26, 27).

The establishment of the position of the Sichuan Embroidery school as the most famous one leaves no room for doubt. The *Records of the Grand Historian (Shi Ji)* writes that Sichuan Province developed silk-weaving industry thanks to popular silkworm-breeding. In the Spring and Autumn Period, people in Sichuan Province were already trading their silk-woven products with present-day Thailand, which created necessary conditions for the emergence of embroidery. In the Eastern Jin Dynasty and Western Jin Dynasty, Sichuan Embroidery, *Shu* brocade, gold, silver, gem, and jade were reputed as treasures of Sichuan. In the wake of the Tang Dynasty, there had been great demands for Sichuan Embroidery among royal family

FIG. 28　*Five Children Striving for the Champion*
It is a frameless embroidered article of Sichuan Embroidery in the Qing Dynasty preserved in the Museum of Sichuan Province.

members and people of all walks of life, hence making it famous across the country. In the Qing Dynasty, Sichuan Embroidery became outstanding from among those kinds of embroidery of local production. At that time, noted painters got involved with the design of the embroidery. Painters and embroiderers worked together, having constantly enhanced the art and techniques of Sichuan Embroidery. Thanks to its prosperity, Sichuan Embroidery naturally developed into one of the four famous schools in China (FIG. 28).

The formation of Hunan Embroidery was also inevitable due to its long history. In the Warring States Period, chain stitch of embroidery was frequently seen in Hunan Province. With a history of over two thousand years, it is marked by vivid patterns and meticulous craftsmanship. In the Song Dynasty and the Ming Dynasty, patterns and needlework of Hunan Embroidery became

FIG. 29　*Lion, Deer, Elephant and Horse*
Embroidery on White Satin
Late Qing Dynasty
Hunan Embroidery of Wu Caixia's Embroidery Workshop
Museum of Hunan Province
It is one of the representatives of Hunan Embroidery in early days.

The establishment of Wu Caixia's embroidery workshop was closely associated with the name of Hu Lianxian (1832–1899), the founder of Hunan Embroidery. Born in Anhui Province, Hu Lianxian later moved to settle down in Suzhou together with her father. She began to learn Suzhou Embroidery during her childhood in addition to painting, which she was very good at. After marrying, she went to live in Xiangyin of Hunan Province together with her husband. Her two sons set up Wu Caixia's Embroidery Workshop in Changsha, which started to become famous across China.

FIG. 30 *Phoenix Facing the Sun*
Guangzhou Embroidery
With classic patterns of Guangzhou Embroidery, this embroidered article has a typical style of the region's embroidery. It is popular among people thanks to its connotation of auspiciousness, joyful celebration, blessing, and happiness. The phoenix is encircled by birds of various postures, along with the sun, clouds, Chinese parasol, peony, magnolia, purple vine, lotus flower, and camellia in reasonable space-distribution of immense magnificence. Embroiderers of Guangzhou Embroidery are good at leaving behind water-paths (i.e. empty fringe-lines), forming a bustling scene marked by clear veins, bright colors, and distinctive layers.

increasingly mature, quite similar to its style nowadays. In the Qing Dynasty, Hunan Embroidery was seen all over the rural and urban areas of the province, with noted embroiderers coming into being successively (FIG. 29). As pointed out by some art connoisseurs in the Qing Dynasty, Hunan Embroidery was free from the manuscripts of Chinese paintings. Instead, it underwent revision according to the needs of embroidery craftsmanship. As a result, works of Hunan Embroidery not only kept the strong points of paintings, but also gave better play to the beauty and exquisiteness of embroidery, hence having formed a unique style of art.

Guangdong Embroidery, including Guangzhou Embroidery and Chaozhou Embroidery, also has a fairly long history. Guangzhou Embroidery is fond of applying strong colors, prosperous scenes to bring about a joyful and bustling atmosphere (FIG. 30). Chaozhou Embroidery is featured by gold thread couching stitch, forming an unrestrained and bold bas-relief effect, which is different from other kinds of embroidery. The craftsmanship of embroidery in Guangdong Province in the Tang Dynasty was already quite extraordinary. In the mid-Ming Dynasty, thanks to convenient transportation of costal trade in Guangdong Province, Guangdong Embroidery became world-famous. For a period of time, Guangdong-embroidered articles were reputed as "Chinese gifts for the West." Works of Guangdong Embroidery are preserved in British, French, German, and American museums, having promoted the popularity and development of embroidery in British and French royal courts (FIG. 31).

FIG. 31 Fan Cases
Guangdong Embroidery
It was sold for RMB 18,000 at the China Guardian Auction Block in spring, 2005.

FIG. 32 *Dragon*
It is a Chaozhou Embroidery article preserved in Beijing Shao Xiaocheng Embroidery Research Institute.

8. World-Wide Influence of Chinese Embroidery

Both the eastern Asian area, which has always been under the influence of Chinese culture, and Europe, which has been connecting with China due to water and land routes of the Silk Road since the Han Dynasty, were overwhelmed by the long history and exquisite craftsmanship of Chinese embroidery that has made desirable contributions to international culture and art.

In the thousand years since the Han Dynasty, ringing camel bells on the land route of the Silk Road as well as the rise and fall of the sails on the water route have been bearing natural resources from China, linking the civilizations of the Orient and the West.

Also starting from the Han Dynasty, Chinese silkworm breeding and techniques of embroidery were spread to Japan, a close neighboring country of China. In the Tang Dynasty, the dragon robe of the emperor of Japan at that time was basically the same as that of the Chinese emperor, i.e. red fabrics were embroidered with Twelve Symbols of Sovereignty, such as the sun, the moon, the star, mountain, and pheasant, with the same connotation. In the Edo period in Japan, Japanese females of the samurai class often wore long robes with motifs of Chinese classic literature. It is not too much to say that Japanese traditional embroidery art is deeply influenced by China, whether in terms of embroidery techniques or themes for embroidery creation.

During the reign of Emperor Qianlong in the Qing Dynasty (1711–1799), hoops of Chinese embroidery were spread to Britain and France, etc., having replaced iron and wooden slate frames and promoted the development of small embroidered crafts.

As believed by Western scholars of art history, Chaozhou Embroidery, a branch of Guangdong Embroidery as one of the four famous embroidery schools in China, as well as gold inlaid painting on Chinese lacquerware, exerted a major influence on art tendencies in Europe, such as European paintings and handicrafts in the 17th and 18th century. European oil paintings displaying the magnificent lives of the imperial court drew on the techniques of embroidery by means of gold and silver threads, using golden color to bring about major outlines, give prominence to the theme and demonstrate bright light. In the field of architecture, Chaozhou Embroidery also exerted an influence on famous Rococo art style which was portrayed with lots of gold threads (FIG. 32).

In modern times, Chinese embroidery has been an important commodity for European merchants to conduct trade in the Far East. There are not only ordinary embroidered crafts from China that were mass produced for export, but also high-grade embroidered works with family crest ordered by aristocrats.

FIG. 33 *Mountain-Magpies and Loquats*
by Shao Xiaocheng (Part)
Song Dynasty Embroidery
Private Collection, USA
Embroidery for appreciation in the
Song Dynasty used the needle as the
pen and the silk as the color. Those
embroidered in great detail without
any stitch traces are of high quality,
and the tail-feather of this blue magpie
is a case in point. Such techniques
of embroidery are even hardly seen
among embroiderers with working
experience of over ten years. A qualified
embroiderer should not only have solid
basic skills, but also profound artistic
attainments in painting.

CHAPTER TWO
TOOLS AND MATERIALS OF EMBROIDERY AND THEIR APPLICATION

The most desirable tool is required if the work needs to be done perfectly. Therefore, in the preparation stage we need to acquire an all-around understanding of embroidery tools and materials. The forms of tools, the selection of materials, and the ways to apply them introduced in this chapter are valuable traditional Chinese embroidery knowledge.

Embroiderers would feel light-hearted, pleasant, and relaxed if tools are handy and easy for operation. So, according to respective circumstances, tools should be convenient, simple, handy, and appropriate as the basic principles for tool-selection. It needs to be pointed out that a complete set of tools and materials is not a must. If embroiderers have no idea about which one to choose, they would find themselves in a troublesome situation.

In this chapter, we also introduce some methods of producing special threads. Unexpected good results would be achieved if embroiderers feel like trying novel materials.

1. Tools

Hoop
Small hoops are mostly used in repairing holes on high-grade garments, while big hoops are used for turning out embroidered articles for daily use (FIG. 34).

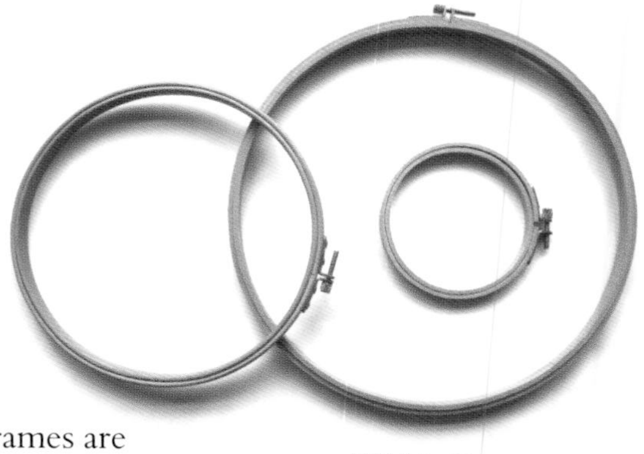

FIG. 34   Hoop

Frame
They are used to make fabrics flat and stretchable. Frames are composed of two horizontal bars, two slats, two pieces of frame-cloth, two pegs, two pieces of thin paper-stripes, and some strings (FIG. 35).

Arm-Rest and Stands
Arm-rest is usually placed on frames. Embroiderers can put their arms on them at work to prevent arm-fatigue.

Stands are specially used to hold frames. Usually, two stands are used. Please choose appropriate stand-height according to the height of the embroiderers (FIG. 36).

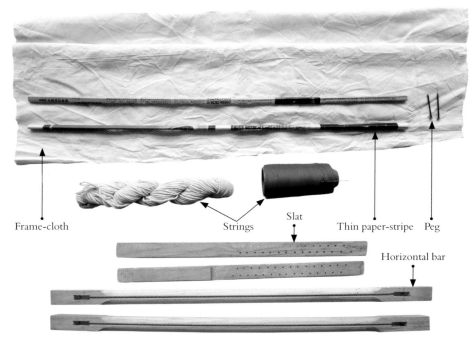

FIG. 35   Parts of a frame

Frame-cloth   Strings   Slat   Thin paper-stripe   Peg

Horizontal bar

FIG. 36   Stands, arm-rest and the embroiderer's posture

Arm-rest   Frame   Stands

FIG. 37   Pattern transfer tools
From the left to the right: Chinese painting pigments, Chinese ink and a small porcelain plate, a pencil, a ball-point pen, a Chinese writing brush, and carbon paper.

Pattern Transfer

"Painting goes before embroidery" is the usual practice. Pattern transfer refers to the fact that patterns first drawn on paper are duplicated on the fabrics before embroidery work (FIG. 37).

Embroidery Needle

9#–12# needles are frequently used since embroidery needles in Chinese embroidery are small and fine. The bigger the numbers of the needles, the finer these needles are. Please choose needles of appropriate size according to the fabrics, needlework, and thickness of embroidery threads, i.e. the thicker the embroidery threads, the smaller the number of the needles, while the thinner the embroidery threads, the bigger the number of needles. Never use too much strength or embroidery needles would bend (FIG. 38).

FIG. 38   Embroidery needles
Embroidery needles are divided into big needle eyes and small needle eyes with respective features. The big-eye embroidery needle makes it easy for the thread to go through, whereas no trace can be found on the fabrics after the small-eye embroidery needle is used.

From the left to the right: Dongfeng 8# needle (27 mm long and 0.6 mm in diameter), Dongfeng 9# needle (25 mm long and 0.5 mm in diameter), Dongfeng 9# long needle (35 mm long and 0.5 mm in diameter), KIRBY's Ne Plus Needles 11# big-eye needle (24 mm long and 0.4 mm in diameter), PONY Sewing Needles 12# small-eye needle (22.5 mm long and 0.35 mm in diameter), Dongfeng 12# needle (25 mm long and 0.45 mm in diameter) and Dongfeng 27# needle for threading beads (56 mm long and 0.6 mm in diameter).

Embroidery Scissors

It would be appropriate for embroidery scissors to be small and sharp. One kind of embroidery scissors has flat tips while another kind has curved tips. Flat-tip embroidery scissors are suitable for cutting off embroidery threads, while curved-tip embroidery scissors are suitable for cutting off threads in the course of embroidery and to trim irregular thread-ends on the bottom of fabrics after the embroidery is completed. In the course of embroidering, it is both handy and good for the surface of fabrics if embroidery scissors are put on the frame-surface (FIG. 39).

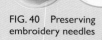

FIG. 39   Embroidery scissors
From the left to the right: curved-tip embroidery scissors and flat-tip embroidery scissors.

Maintenance of Embroidery Needles and Embroidery Scissors

The longer the needle is used, the smoother the surface of the needle is, and the handier the needle is. Therefore, while using needles, pay attention to keeping your hands clean to prevent dirty spots on the embroidered article due to rusty needles. If needles are not used for the time being, they should be put into talcum powder cases to prevent them from air exposure, so as to ensure their smoothness and dryness. It is not appropriate to insert needles into a pincushion in order to prevent rust (FIG. 40).

FIG. 40   Preserving embroidery needles

Tips of embroidery scissors should be well protected. Please don't use them to cut hard things or things which may damage their blade. When they are not used, please smear a little sewing machine oil on them (this is not necessary for stainless-steel embroidery scissors) and put them into a scissor bag. Sewing machine oil should be wiped if they are used again so as not to make embroidery threads and fabrics dirty (FIG. 41).

FIG. 41   Preserving embroidery scissors

2. Materials

Embroidery Threads

There is a wide variety of embroidery threads, such as silk, wool, cotton, and chemical fiber threads, etc.

Frequently-used threads in Chinese embroidery are:

Silk threads. They look bright and decorative, with their special tint best expressing the effect of animal furs. They can be divided but are vulnerable to washing and sunlight due to weak strength.

Gold and silver threads. They are threads chiefly made of gold and silver as well as their imitations. Application of gold and silver threads gives rise to the magnificent style of embroidery. However, due to their fragile texture, they are not suitable for complicated needlework.

Cotton threads. They are made of combed cotton, marked by high strength, bright colors, complete color variety, resistance against washing and sunlight, and freedom from fluffs. Cotton threads are usually used on cotton and linen fabrics, enjoying quite extensive application.

Sewing threads. They are made of polyester fiber marked by high strength, tenacity, various colors, and colors of different grades, hence making them applicable to a variety of themes on different embroidered articles. They can also be used to couch gold threads.

Hair threads. As a special kind of material for hair embroidery, they have such natural tints as black, white, grey, yellow, and brown. Besides, tough, smooth, and fine, they are able to keep the tint for a long time. Therefore, embroidered works based on hair are featured by fine and dense needlework as well as soft color in a unique style.

Fabrics

There is a wide variety of fabrics which are divided into such kinds as silk, cotton, and linen as raw materials, in addition to many sorts of fabrics with blended textures. While choosing fabrics, one should take comprehensive account of the functions, contents, embroidery schools, and needlework. Fine, dense, smooth, and clean embroidery is a must. Fabrics of undesirable quality would affect the color of embroidered articles (FIG. 42).

Preservation of Silk Threads

Silk contains such organic substances as protein. It is not appropriate to keep too much of it since it is apt to decay along with the elapse of time. So, it is advisable to buy it when it is intended to be used. Kraft paper can be used to preserve silk threads. Kraft paper is first cut into oblong shape. Its width is equal to the length of a roll of silk threads. Silk threads are placed flat on the well-cut kraft paper according to the colors and their shades, and then bound up by fine strings. After that, rolls upon rolls of silk threads are put neatly in the cabinet for future use.

Preservation of other kinds of embroidery threads can refer to the preservation of silk threads. Mind you that silk threads should be put at the place free from dust, moisture and strong light.

According to the different embroidery schools, the frequently-used fabrics are:

A. Fabrics Suitable for Single-Sided Embroidery

Real silk satin damask. Flat, smooth, and shiny, they are thicker than plain crepe satin. Due to their reasonable price and extensive use, they are suitable both for turning out embroidered articles for daily use and articles for appreciation.

Plain crepe satin. With bright surface, sleek, and smooth feelings, it is slightly thinner than real silk satin damask. However, it drapes more obviously and feels much better. Plain crepe satin is often used to produce such high-grade daily necessities of soft texture as scarves, handkerchiefs, and fashion clothes.

Pure cotton cloth. Marked by desirable absorption of moisture and permeability, it is glossless, quite soft, firm, durable, and easy to wash, making it suitable to turn out embroidery of popular garments and garments of ethnic minorities. It would be more desirable if cotton embroidery threads are used.

Cotton linen fabrics. Blended with cotton and linen, with a thick texture, it is more suitable for embroidery with cotton threads, just like pure cotton cloth.

Silk cloth. As the general term for silk fabrics, it is seldom used on the daily use embroidery and often used for appreciation embroidery.

Plain woven silk fabrics. With a thick texture but without the brightness, cleanness, and gorgeousness of satin damask, it is relatively durable for washing.

B. Fabrics Suitable for Double-Sided Embroidery

Real silk voile. It is featured by lightness, thinness, and transparency. In addition, it feels flat, erect, and slightly hard. Its fabrics are more transparent and thinner than thin silk tabby.

Real silk tabby. It looks like raw silk, but more compact. In comparison, it is opaque with antique and simple colors.

C. Fabrics Suitable for High-Quality Embroidered Calligraphy and Paintings

Real silk taffeta. With fine, dense, light, and thin surface, it is marked by even and erect texture in addition to elegant tints and soft gloss. As silk fabrics of very high grade, it is usually used for producing high-grade embroidery.

D. Fabrics Suitable for Counted Stitch over Gauze Embroidery and Woolen Embroidery

Real silk gauze. With light and transparent texture, it has interwoven square holes.

Jute mixed-woven cloth. It has mesh and feels heavy.

Real silk satin damask

Plain crepe satin

Real silk voile

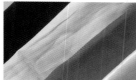
Real silk tabby

Silk cloth

Plain woven silk fabrics

Real silk taffeta

Real silk gauze and jute mixed-woven cloth

FIG. 42 Embroidery fabrics

3. Basic Techniques for Application

Start and Finish Off the Embroidery

The embroidery thread between the point where the needle is brought up and the point where the needle is inserted is commonly called a stitch. The length of this part of the embroidery thread is the length of the stitch.

In Chinese embroidery, knotting is not often used. At the beginning of an embroidery project and when it is completed, the thread end is often fixed by a few very short running stitches so that there will be no knot on the reverse side. It is usually applied to embroidery for appreciation to ensure the exquisiteness of the embroidered article and further smoothness of mounting.

Hoop the Work

It is aimed at making the fabrics smooth, wrinkle-free for the convenience of embroidery.

1 Sew the fabric with the frame-cloth. The embroidery fabric should be sewn right in the middle.

2 Put the fabric and the frame-cloth on the horizontal bars. Set aside a 2-cm fringe of the frame-cloth as the outer part. Fill the space of the horizontal bars with thin paper-stripes so as to fix the frame-cloth.

3 Roll the frame-cloth of both sides onto the horizontal bars and straighten them.

4 Insert the slats into one side of the horizontal bars respectively to straighten the fabric.

5 Insert the pegs respectively into the hole at the each end of the slat to fix the frame on one side. The same method is used to handle the slat on the other side. Pegs should be respectively inserted into the same position of the slats on both sides so as to ensure that the frame is kept in a right way without any slant.

6 Sew triangle thread-circles with fairly thick sewing threads on one side of the fabric. First, start sewing from one end and then to the other end. The distance between two stitches is about 3 cm.

7 With this done, start sewing back from one end to the other end, hence forming a number of triangle thread-circles. Apply the same method to the other side. The number of triangle thread-circles on each side should be the same.

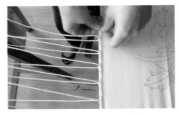

8 Interweave the strings in order to connect the fabric with the slats.

9 First, vertically stretch and tighten the fabric. Then, horizontally pull and tighten the strings, fixing the fabric onto the slats. Thus, the fabric is stretched flatly on the frame, leading to the completion.

Pattern Transfer

Patterns are usually drawn on the paper prior to embroidery. Then, patterns on the drawings are transferred to the embroidery fabrics. There are two kinds of pattern transfer: transferring by carbon paper is suitable for turning out small embroidered articles of daily life (see steps 1–3 below). Transferring by light is suitable for big embroidered articles of high quality (see steps 4–6 below).

1 Place the fabric flatly on the clean table. Then put the drawing on the fabric.

2 Put the carbon paper under the drawing. Use the paper weight to press the fabric and the drawing. Use the pen to trace the outline of the patterns on the drawing. Thus, the drawing is transferred onto the fabric.

3 Completed.

4 Reverse the frame. Reverse the drawing and stick it to the frame with adhesive tape.

5 Turn the frame upside down and place it on a light box. Through the light, you can see the drawing below the fabric. Then, use a writing brush to outline the pattern with light ink. Thus, patterns are transferred onto the fabric.

6 Take away the drawing. According to original artwork, apply a layer of light color onto the patterns on the fabric with various pigments of Chinese painting with colors that are not going to easily fade. If the embroiderer is well grounded in painting, he does not have to add colors to the fabrics.

Dividing the Thread Strands

In Chinese embroidery, silk threads are usually divided into finer strands for use. The more strands the threads are divided into, the more exquisite the embroidered articles are. In doing so, ten fingers should coordinate with one another, with appropriate strength used.

With half of the thread drawn out first, hold one end of the thread between the middle finger and the fourth finger of your left hand, pick up the thread with your index finger and hold the other end of the thread with your right hand. While keeping the original posture with your left hand, you can hold the thread with your middle finger, use your thumbnail to direct at the place where the thread is held by your middle finger and pinch the middle of the thread. Then use your right hand to hold the other end of the thread to flick them slightly, separating the threads pinched by the thumb of your left hand. Please note that the original posture of the left hand should be kept intact.

Use your thumb and index finger on your right hand to hold one end of the thread while using your middle finger to get into the separated threads, slightly and slowly splitting the threads along the place where threads are separated. The number of threads divided is in accordance with the need. The above mentioned process of operation requires appropriate strength. Only by repeated practice, can smooth, filament-free, and tenacious silk threads be proficiently divided.

1 An entire embroidery thread is used.

2 Usually, a thin thread can be divided into 16 strands, with 8 strands for half of the thread.

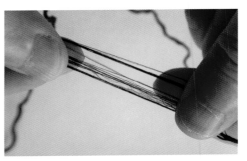

3 Usually, a thick thread can be divided into 80 strands.

Making Special Threads

The wide variety of embroidery threads is one of the important reasons for the changeable and rich styles of Chinese embroidery. Apart from various embroidery threads mentioned above, animal hair and ordinary embroidery threads are also used to turn out some special threads for embroidery.

A. Plait-Weaving Threads

Some threads of the same color are used to weave "plaits" before they are applied to embroidery. There are plait-weaving with seven threads, nine threads or twelve threads, etc. Plait-weaving with nine threads is taken as an example as follows to explain the plait-weaving methods.

1 Encircle nine threads onto nine poles respectively, with five threads on the right and four threads on the left.

2 Take the first thread on your right. Weaving takes place on top of one thread and below the next thread towards the left side; i.e. put the first thread on top of the second and then below the third thread, so on and so forth. When the first thread advances to the middle space between the left and the right groups of nine threads, put it into the original left group with four threads. At this time, there are five threads in the group on the left and four threads in the group on the right.

Then, take the first thread on your left. Weaving takes place on top of one thread and below the next thread towards the right side. When the first thread advances to the middle space between the left and the right groups, put this thread into the original right group with four threads. At this time, there are five threads in the group on the right and four threads in the group on the left. Afterwards, weaving takes place from the right to the left repeatedly, so on and so forth. When certain length is reached in weaving, it should be fixed onto the upper part of an object for further weaving, until the required length is reached.

B. Horse-Tail-Hair Threads

They are quite hard since horse tail is wrapped by silk threads, and patterns outlined with horse-tail-hair threads tend to stay unchanged. Oil in the horse tail is conducive to maintain the gloss of the outlying silk threads. Those embroidered articles with this kind of threads are strong and durable (FIG. 43).

FIG. 43   How to make horse-tail-hair threads

Use one or several pieces of horse-tail hairs as core threads. Encircle the silk threads around the core threads in a spiral way. While doing so, one should pay attention to using hand-strength in an even manner.

A 90-degree angle should be kept between silk threads and core threads. It is better not to reveal the horse-tail hair. Sometimes, palm fibers are also used as core threads. The same method is applied in producing palm fiber threads.

C. Peacock-Feather Threads

Peacock-feathers wrapped by silk threads are twisted into embroidery threads, making embroidered articles gorgeous and eye-catching.

1 Take off the peacock feathers grown symmetrically on both sides of the tail one piece after another.

Cut off the white parts at the root of peacock feathers. Put the peacock feathers on the white paper for future use. Choose silk threads or cotton threads with colors similar to those of peacock feathers.

2 Twist the silk thread with a piece of peacock feather. Connect the peacock feathers one after another as twisting goes on. When certain length is reached, encircle the twisted peacock-feather threads around a thread reel. Then, there goes the same method continuously, until all peacock-feather threads are twisted.

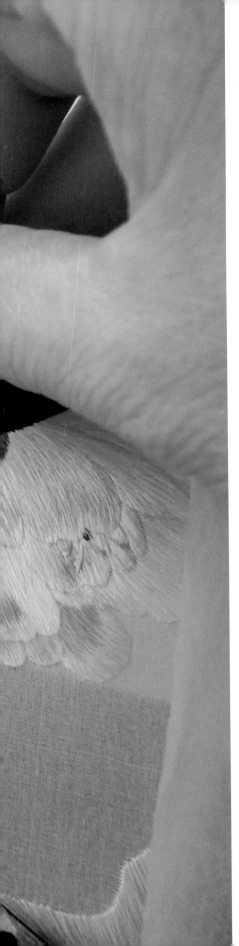

CHAPTER THREE
CHINESE EMBROIDERY NEEDLEWORK

In China, the evolution and development of embroidery techniques have been ongoing. With their wisdom and intelligence, handicraftsmen have created a variety of needlework in the process of bringing changes to each stitch, each piece of thread and each piece of cloth. In this chapter, we will introduce twenty-five kinds of Chinese embroidery needlework.

Simple needlework first developed before the appearance of more complex and exquisite needlework through gradual refinement. For Chinese embroidery during the earliest time, mono-needlework was able to bring about embroidery independently. In the following periods, a variety of needlework was applied to one piece of work, often making the picture more detailed with richer artistic expression.

In this chapter, you will also see around twenty pieces of works solely produced by one needlework, i.e. petals produced by shaded satin stitch appear vivid and extremely gorgeous; "daisies" produced by free cross stitch look very decorative in a strong local style; the embroidery article entitled "bamboo and flower roundel" produced by knot stitch is marked by antiquity, simplicity, boldness, and vigor.

FIG. 44　Embroidering the hibiscus flower
Embroidery should be handled gently and agilely, with harmonious coordination of all ten fingers. Proficient operation requires the combination of eyes, the mind, and two hands. The hand holding the needle often appears in the shape of an orchid, with the center of the palm being hollow. Along with the rise and the fall of the hand, the air flows across the palm, enabling the hand to be clean and dry, hence leading to the brightness of the article embroidered.

1. Running Stitch

As one of the needleworks applied to fabrics very early, it is featured by fairly short stitches just like little beads. Despite its simplicity and explicitness, it can bring about quite different patterns of embroidery through various designs.

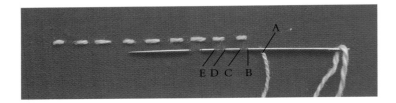

Bring out the needle at A and pull out the whole thread. Insert the needle at B and immediately bring it out at C. Then insert the needle at D and immediately bring it out at E. Always keep the needle in and out along the line being stitched. Be sure that the stitches are equal in length.

Variation

In the course of embroidery, the stitch can be long or short, forming different geometirc patterns. Or the stitch can be of equal length, but the rows of stitches are arranged alternately to form different patterns.

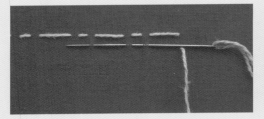

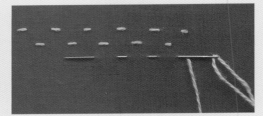

The application of a long running stitch and then a short one has brought changes to the simple needlework.

The first and second rows of running stitch being arranged alternately makes the pattern look more vivid.

Flowers

Following the pattern on the left, use pink and purple threads to embroider flowers, while green threads of different shades are applied to embroider leaves and stalks.

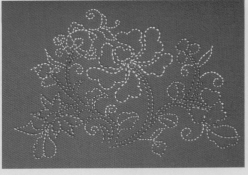

2. Chain Stitch

In the period from the Warring States to the Han Dynasty more than 2,000 years ago, chain stitch was quite commonly seen. It was named because it looks like a chain. This needlework is marked by evenness and firmness, suitable for revealing smooth and sleek lines while its dense array also makes it appear decent thanks to the effect of texture, in addition to its simplicity for mastery. No stretching is required during embroidery and it can be directly embroidered by hand.

There are three kinds of chain stitch, i.e. closed chain stitch, open chain stitch, and ancient chain stitch.

Closed Chain Stitch

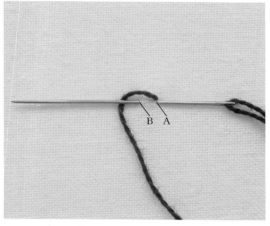

1 Bring the needle out at A and pull out the whole thread. Insert the needle beside A and then bring the needle out immediately at B. Loop the thread beneath the needle when the needle comes out.

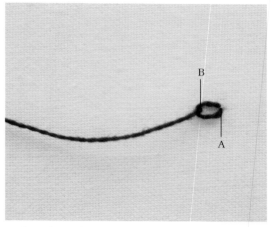

2 Bring the needle out to pull out the whole thread. Tighten the loop and adjust. The first loop of the chain is finished.

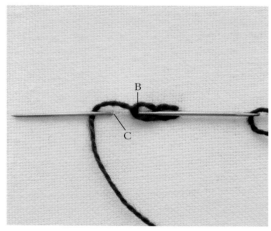

3 Insert the needle beside B which is inside the first loop and then immediately bring out the needle at C. Loop the thread beneath the needle when the needle comes out. Bring out the needle and pull out the whole thread. Tighten the loop and adjust. The second loop of the chain is finished.

4 Repeat and continue to complete the rest of the loops of the chain. An example of closed chain stitch.

Open Chain Stitch

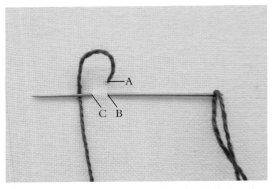

1 Bring out the needle at A and pull out the whole thread. Insert the needle at B below A before bringing out the needle immediately at C. Loop the thread beneath the needle when the needle comes out. The distance between A and B is equal to the size of the opening.

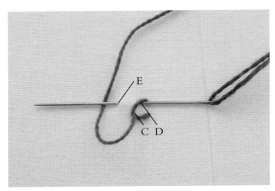

2 Bring out the needle and pull out the whole thread. Tighten the loop and adjust. The first loop of the chain is completed. Then insert the needle at D above C inside the loop and bring out the needle immediately at E. Loop the thread beneath the needle when the needle comes out. Be sure that the distance between C and D is equal to that between A and B.

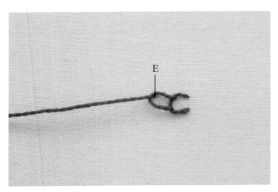

3 Bring out the needle and pull out the whole thread. Tighten the loop and adjust. The second loop of the chain is completed.

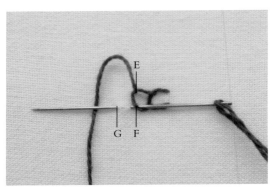

4 Insert the needle at F right below E inside the second loop and bring out the needle immediately at G. Loop the thread beneath the needle when it comes out. Be sure that the distance between E and F is equal to that of A and B as well as between C and D.

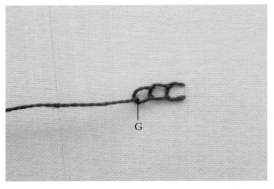

5 Bring out the needle and pull out the whole thread. Tighten the loop and adjust. The third loop is completed.

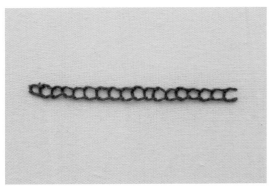

6 The procedure continues like this all the way to repeat the preceding method of stitch. An example of open chain stitch.

Ancient Chain Stitch

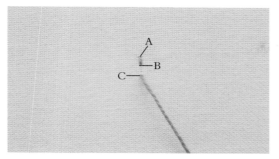

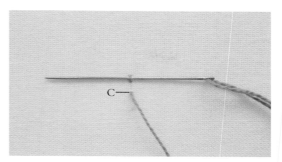

1 Bring out the needle at A and pull out the whole thread. Insert the needle at B and bring out it at C. Pull out the whole thread.

2 Pass the needle under the stitch of A and B. Insert the needle beside C.

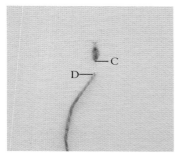

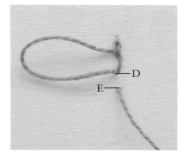

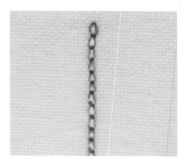

3 Bring out the needle and pull out the whole thread. Tighten the loop and adjust. The first loop is completed. Then bring out the needle at D.

4 Pass the needle under the stitch between B and C and insert it at D. The second loop is completed. Then bring out the needle at E.

5 Repeat and continue to complete the rest of the loops of the chain. An example of ancient chain stitch.

Phoenix

You can try to apply the ancient chain stitch to embroider the phoenix on the right by following the pattern on the left.

3. Straight Satin Stitch

Straight satin stitch can be traced back to the Western Han Dynasty (206 BC–25 AD).

It is composed of vertical lines. Its short and dense stitch-lines can fully cover embroidery fabrics and even bring about patterns independently. In the course of embroidery, threads advance toward the same direction, with even fringes and mono-color. If such stitch is applied to fully cover the fabric, it's better to use plain woven cloth whose meridian and parallel lines are visible. Stitches can follow the cloth-veins in the process of embroidery. The thickness of the cloth is decided by the design style of patterns.

Bring the needle out at A and insert the needle at B. Pull out the whole thread and tighten it. Then bring the needle up at C and insert the needle at D. AB should be closely attached to CD on a par. Such process goes on repeatedly until patterns are completed.

Patterns of Rectangular Spirals and Cross-Shaped Flowers

Such patterns are embroidered by straight satin stitch according to the patterns on the sketch.

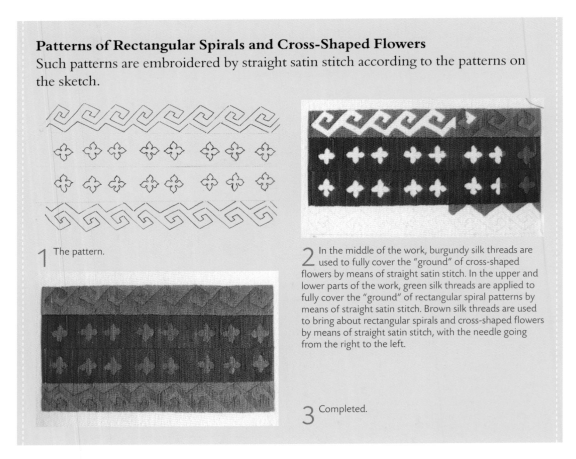

1 The pattern.

2 In the middle of the work, burgundy silk threads are used to fully cover the "ground" of cross-shaped flowers by means of straight satin stitch. In the upper and lower parts of the work, green silk threads are applied to fully cover the "ground" of rectangular spiral patterns by means of straight satin stitch. Brown silk threads are used to bring about rectangular spirals and cross-shaped flowers by means of straight satin stitch, with the needle going from the right to the left.

3 Completed.

4. Blanket Stitch

Similar to bringing out button holes on a garment, it was applied to embroidery as early as the Eastern Han Dynasty. Now, it is frequently seen in the embroidery of the Miao ethnic minority in China and sometimes in the embroidery attached with cloth of the Han in China. With the most basic skills mastered, blanket stitch of different shapes can be brought about by following the different outlines of the patterns required.

Basic Blanket Stitch

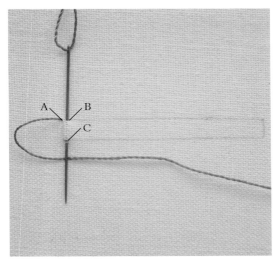

1 Bring out the needle at A and bring out the whole thread. Insert the needle at B near A and then bring it out immediately at C with the thread pressed under the needle.

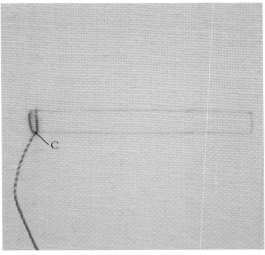

2 Pull out the needle to bring out the whole thread and then tighten it to complete the first stitch.

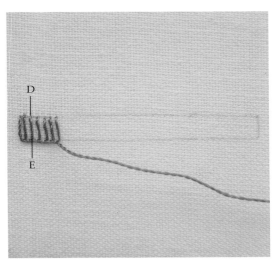

3 Insert the needle at D and then bring it out immediately at E with the thread pressed under the needle. Pull out the needle and the whole thread and tighten it to complete the second stitch.

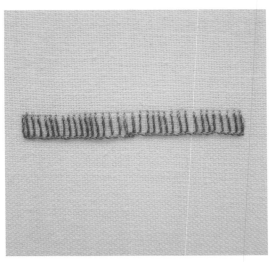

4 The embroidery goes on with the same method. Completed.

Long and Short Blanket Stitch

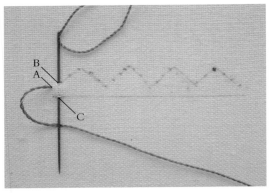

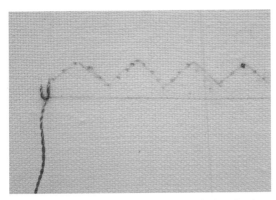

1 Bring out the needle at A to pull out the whole thread. Insert the needle at B and then bring it out immediately at C with the thread pressed under the needle.

2 Pull out the needle and bring out the whole thread and tighten it to complete the first stitch.

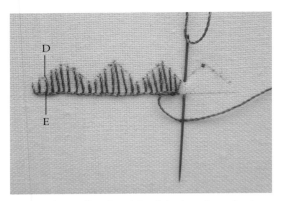

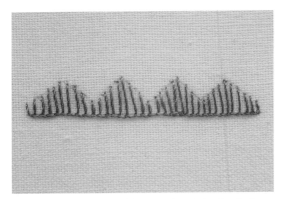

3 Insert the needle at D and then bring it out immediately at E with the thread pressed under the needle. Pull out the needle to bring out the whole thread and tighten it to complete the second stitch. The embroidery goes on with the same method.

4 With regular changes of length in the stitches for the lower part, you can bring about any shape you wish. Completed.

Curved Blanket Stitch

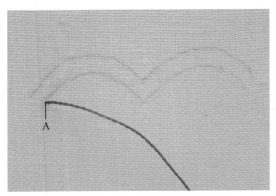

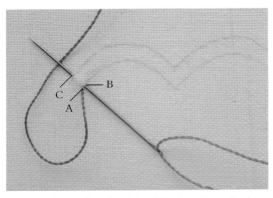

1 Bring the needle out at A and pull out the whole thread.

2 Insert the needle at B and then bring it out immediately at C with the thread pressed under the needle.

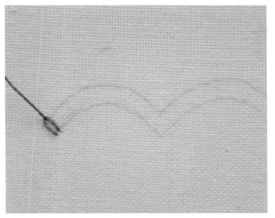

3 Pull out the needle to bring out the whole thread and tighten it to complete the first stitch.

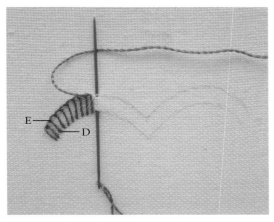

4 Insert the needle at D and then bring it out immediately at E with the thread pressed under the needle. Pull out the needle and bring out the whole thread and tighten it to complete the second stitch.

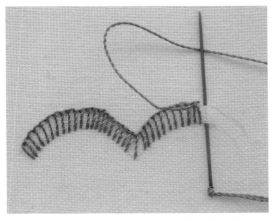

5 The same method is applied to embroidery along the already sketched arc.

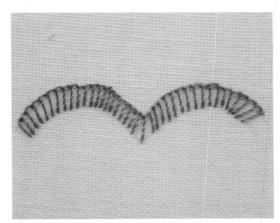

6 Completed.

Flower Pattern Blanket Stitch

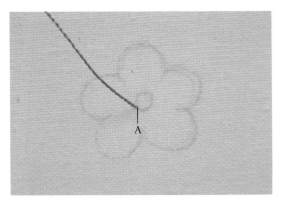

1 Bring the needle out at A to pull out the whole thread.

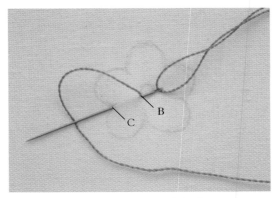

2 Insert the needle at B close to A and then bring it out immediately at C with the thread pressed under the needle.

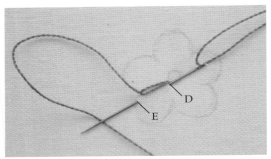

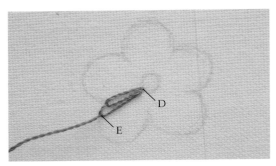

3 Pull out the needle to bring out the whole thread and tighten it to complete the first stitch. Insert the needle at D close to B and then bring it out immediately at E with the thread pressed under the needle.

4 Pull out the needle to bring out the whole thread and tighten it to complete the second stitch.

5 The same method is applied to embroidery along the already sketched arc to complete the first petal.

6 Be sure the circle representing the stamen in the middle that each stitch must be closely linked. Only by doing so can we spread petals in a radiated way.

7 Completed.

Gorgeous Flowers

The needlework of each part:

  Petals: curved blanket stitch

  The stamen at the center: flower pattern blanket stitch

  The stamen of flowers around: long and short blanket stitch

5. Stem Stitch

This needlework follows the curved line of patterns through connection. Threads for such embroidery should be fine and the length of the stitches should be arranged properly to make the lines flowing, natural, and vivid.

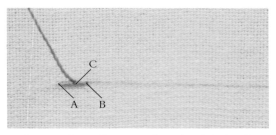

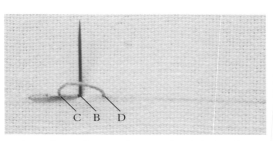

1 Bring out the needle at A to pull out the whole thread. Insert the needle at B to bring out the whole thread. Be sure the distance between A and B is about 7 mm. Then bring out the needle at C in the middle of AB. Bring out the needle, pull out the whole thread and tighten it. Make sure the stitch is straightened and attached flatly on the embroidery fabric.

2 Insert the needle at D to bring out the whole thread. Be sure the distance between C and D is 7 mm. Then bring out the needle at B in the middle of CD.

3 Bring out the needle to pull out the whole thread and tighten it.

4 The same method is applied to embroidery along the line already sketched to make sure that each stitch is firm and well-attached. Completed.

Cherry Flower Roundel

Based on the pattern on the left, apply the stem stitch to embroider the outer-frame with purple threads, flowers with pink threads, and leaves with green threads.

6. Split Stitch

Similar to stem stitch, it is suitable for embroidering leaves, stems, Chinese characters and bird feathers, etc.

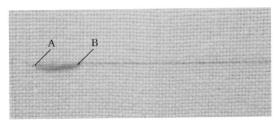

1 Bring out the needle at A and then insert at B. Pull out the whole thread and tighten it. The distance between A and B should be 7 mm.

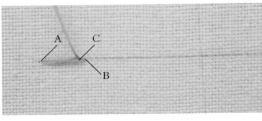

2 Bring out the needle gently at C close to B. Split the thread with the needle tip. Bring out the needle and pull out the whole thread and tighten it.

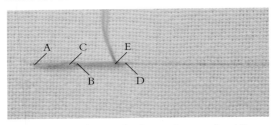

3 Insert the needle at D. The distance between C and D should be 7 mm. Pull out the whole thread and tighten it. Bring out the needle at E close to D. Split the thread with the needle tip. Bring out the needle and pull out the whole thread and tighten it.

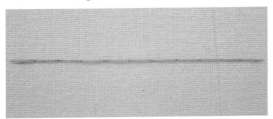

4 The same method is applied to embroidery along the line already sketched. Make sure that the stitch is tightened and well-attached on the embroidery fabric.

7. Bead Work

It is a kind of needlework that applies beads of various colors and forms to the fabrics, presenting a strong sense of three dimensional patterns. Since the Eastern Han Dynasty, Chinese people have been applying beads to embroidery. The beadwork is still popular among people. In order to prevent beads from falling off, the beginning and the end of such embroidery should be knotted and secured.

Bead Work with Stem Stitch

Bring the needle out at A. Slide an appropriate number of beads onto the thread according to the width of petals to be sewn. Insert the needle at B and bring it out immediately at C, which is in the vicinity of A. Straighten the thread. Repeat to continue from one side of the petals to the other following the direction indicated by the arrow.

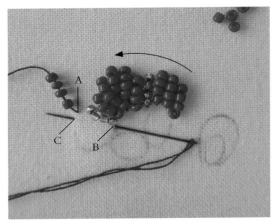

With one petal embroidered, apply the same stitch to work a line of golden beads at the joint of two petals to set them apart. Then work on the second petal.

Please note that the stitch length should be equal to the total length of a number of beads. Shorter stitch length would lead to uneven beads, while longer stitch length would lead to loose beads.

Bead Work with Back Stitch

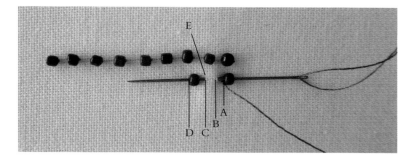

Use the back stitch. Bring the needle out at A and slide in a coffee-color bead. Insert the needle at B. Bring the needle out at C and slide in another bead. Bring out the needle to pull out the whole thread. Insert the needle at D close to C. Couch the bead tightly. Bring out the needle at E which is close to C under the bead. Repeat and continue.

Bead Work with Running Stitch

Bring the needle out at A and slide in a bead-tube. Insert the needle at B and straighten the thread. Then bring the needle out at C and insert the needle at D in the same way. Repeat to continue from one side of the leaf to the other in following the direction indicated by the arrow.

Please note that the stitch length should be equal to the length of the bead-tube. A shorter stitch length would lead to uneven bead-tube, while longer stitch length would lead to loose bead-tubes.

Use the stem stitch to work on the blue beads in order to finish the lower parts of the petals.

Bead Work with Simple Couching Stitch

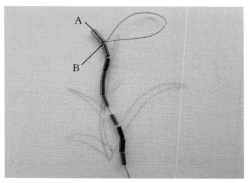

Bring the needle out at A and string enough bead-tubes with the length required by the pattern. Put the bead-tubes onto the fabrics. Bring a second needle strung with another thread and couch over the thread at B amidst two bead-tubes to hold them. Couch over the thread at the interval of every two bead-tubes for curved lines. Couch over the thread at the interval of every two bead-tubes for straight lines to ensure they are smooth. With all bead-tubes fixed, take both two needles to the back of the fabric and finish both threads off securely to completion.

Flower

Bead work for different parts:

Flowers: bead work with stem stitch

The ground: bead work with back stitch

The upper parts of the leaves: bead work with running stitch

The lower parts of the leaves: bead work with stem stitch

The flower stalks: bead work with simple couching stitch

FIG. 45
Two Beauties by
Shao Xiaocheng
Gu-Style Embroidery
Private Collection, Hong Kong,
China

As the representative of southern Chinese embroidery in the Ming Dynasty, Gu-Style is a school of embroidery different from that of Shandong Embroidery in the same period, enjoying an important historical position. This piece of embroidered article was completed by silk threads of medium color, instead of the darkest or the lightest color, so as to ensure that soft and elegant color was applied. The faces of beauties were embroidered with one fine thread and half of a fine thread, while their eye-expression and hair-style were embroidered with one fourth of a thread, making them faintly discernible on the fabric seemingly like painting-trace. Therefore, it has become true "painting-like embroidery."

Historically, in order to achieve more conformity with painting, high-quality Gu-Style Embroidery was first painted before embroidery took place, or embroidery first before painting was done. This piece of embroidered article, entirely completed by needlework without any painting, has brought about the spiritual appeal the same as that of painting. A variety of needlework were applied at one go according to the needs, making it flat, thin, fine and soft. The embroidered surface is attached to the fabric like the painting, making it difficult to tell whether it is embroidery or painting and bringing the artistic style of Gu-Style Embroidery to the peak. This is a piece of high-quality embroidered article marked by some improvement and self-style while inheriting tradition.

8. Encroaching Satin Stitch

Neat straight stitch is applied to embroidery in bands according to the sketch outline, connecting layer after layer from the front to the rear. There is a transition of color in different shades, hence reaching the effect of color-infiltration. Encroaching satin stitch endows embroidered articles with clear color shades, possessing a better decorative effect.

Encroaching satin stitch is divided into three kinds, i.e. basic encroaching satin stitch, interval encroaching satin stitch, and encroaching satin stitch with hidden threads. The basic encroaching satin stitch proceeds downward from the top of the sketch in bands. The interval encroaching satin stitch handles embroidery in different bands. The encroaching satin stitch with hidden threads proceeds upward from the bottom of the sketch and the second band of stitch begins to conceal a horizontal thread in the embroidery threads of straight satin stitch, producing more obvious color shades and three-dimensional effect.

Attention should be paid to the color-transition to avoid disharmony of the color of two neighboring batches under gradual changes.

Basic Encroaching Satin Stitch

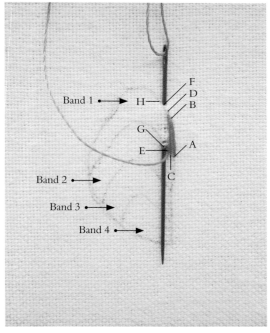

1 The patterns (a petal) are first divided into four bands of roughly the same width. Embroidery begins from the first band at the upper part. First, bring the needle out at A and insert at B. With the needle pulled out, bring out the whole thread and tightened. Bring the needle out at C and insert at D. With the needle pulled out, bring out the whole thread and tightened. Bring the needle out at E and insert at F. With the needle pulled out, bring out the whole thread and tightened. Bring the needle out at G and insert at H. With the needle pulled out, bring out the whole thread and tightened.

2 The procedure goes on like this, leading to the completion of the first band of embroidery. Stitch should be neat and the length is decided by the size of the outline.

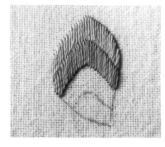

3 Apply the method introduced above to the embroidery of the second band. Be sure that the point of insertion of the second band of stitch should be very close to the inside of the point of the first band of stitches where the needle is brought out (i.e. A, C, E and G), rather than between two stitches. It would come to the third band and the fourth band after the second band is completed.

4 Completed.

Interval Encroaching Satin Stitch

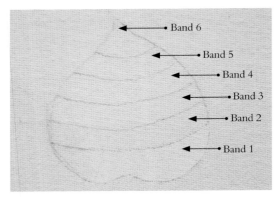

1 The pattern (a peach) is first divided into six bands of roughly the same width.

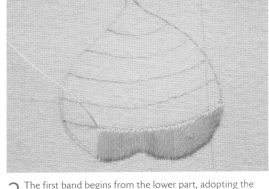

2 The first band begins from the lower part, adopting the first step of the basic encroaching satin stitch.

3 With the second band set aside, the third band comes forward for embroidery, adopting the first step of the basic encroaching satin stitch.

4 With the fourth band set aside, the fifth band comes forward for embroidery, adopting the first step of the basic encroaching satin stitch.

5 For embroidery of the sixth band, the fourth band and the second band starts from the top to the bottom in order. Be sure that the point at which the needle is inserted and brought out should be within the head and end threads of two bands before and after it (i.e. A and B).

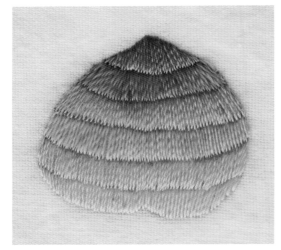

6 There should be no space between the preceding band and the following band. Completed.

Encroaching Satin Stitch with Hidden Threads

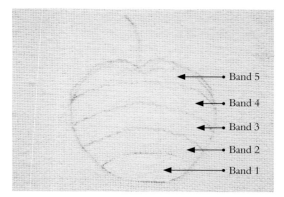

1 The pattern (an apple) is first divided into five bands of roughly the same width.

2 The first band begins from the bottom of the sketch, adopting the first step of the basic encroaching satin stitch.

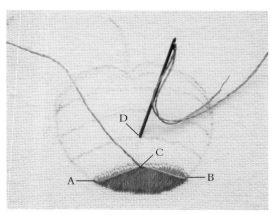

3 Bring the needle out at A and insert at B, bringing about a horizontal line. Then bring the needle out at C (with the horizontal line at the upper part of the needle when it is brought out) and insert at D. With the needle pulled out and the whole thread brought out, the horizontal line is tightened into a herringbone shape.

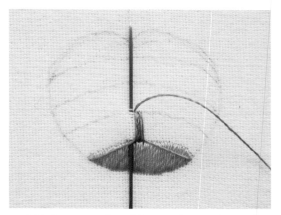

4 With the same method of the second step and CD line as the center, half of the left of the second band should be embroidered. Then return to the CD line, with half of the right of the second band being embroidered. At last, the horizontal line has been turned into an arc and concealed in the embroidery threads at the bottom of the second-band stitches.

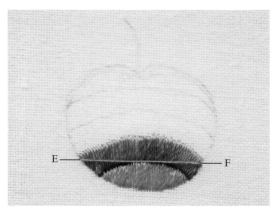

5 With the embroidery of the second band completed, the same method is applied to the embroidery of the third band, the fourth band, and the fifth band.

6 Only with the horizontal line of each band embroidered quite tightly can the embroidery be neat and three-dimensional. Completed.

9. Gold/Silver Thread Couching Stitch

In terms of this needlework, tacking threads are used to fix stiff gold or silver threads on the surface of fabrics. Gold or silver threads cannot be fixed firmly unless tacking threads are used since they are colorful firm sewing threads. Gold or silver threads can also set off the color of tacking threads. When desirable colors of tacking threads are chosen, the unique style of gold/silver thread couching stitch could be more prominent.

This needlework is applied extensively in various Chinese embroidery schools. Slight changes can give embroidered articles special features.

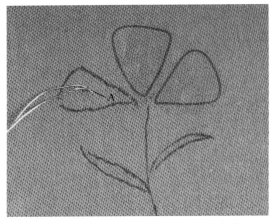

1 Use two strands of gold or silver threads to apply this stitch. Put the end of the gold thread through the needle eye first and then fold it to align both ends of this thread, hence having strung two strands of threads. Bring the needle out at A as the central point of the triangle petal.

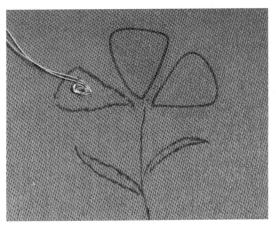

2 Gold thread couching stitch is done from the center outward while they are being tacked. They are triangle petals. Therefore, at the beginning of couching, the direction of gold threads should be set in a triangle manner. While being couched, gold threads should be fixed by red sewing threads with running stitch. Be sure that two strands of gold threads should be respectively tacked with tacking threads at every turns to make it easier to wind.

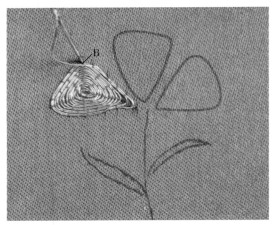

3 Tacking threads should be even with reasonable space in between to make it attractive. With the petals fully couched, insert the needle strung with the gold thread at B and bring the gold thread to the reverse of the fabric to complete the petals.

4 Start to embroider the leaves after the three petals are done. Bring the gold thread out at C as the central point of one leaf. In the wake of it, the gold thread is couched along the outline of the leaf that are tacked by the green threads at the same time.

5 Gold threads are basically a single color. Changing the color of tacking threads can set off the color of gold threads. As shown in the picture, gold threads look green when leaf blades are tacked by green sewing threads, while gold threads look red when the petals are tacked by red sewing threads.

6 With couching done, insert the needle strung with the tacking thread at D between two strands of gold threads. Then two short and small running stitches are sewn in replacement of knotting.

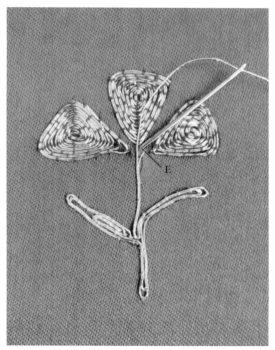

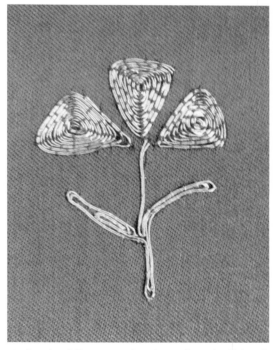

7 When completed, insert the needle strung with the gold thread at E and then bring the gold thread to the reverse of the fabric.

8 Completed. Please note when the couching of gold threads is going on, the needlework with gold threads should continue without a stop.

FIG. 46 *Lions* by Yang Yingxiu (1912–1993) Hunan Embroidery

People in modern times all know that Hunan Embroidery is known for its fierce animals such as tigers, lions, etc. In fact, Hunan Embroidery was not famous for its embroidered lions in the early days, but its more brilliant embroidered articles of Chinese paintings.

This embroidered article integrates painting with embroidery craftsmanship through choice-making and revision, keeping the strong points of the painting while giving better play to the beauty and meticulousness of embroidery in a unique style of Hunan Embroidery.

It was produced in the 1980s, showing the habit and tradition of integrating Chinese embroidery with calligraphy and painting while fully demonstrating the artistic features of Hunan Embroidery.

10. Net Stitch

It is suitable for embroidering geometric net patterns with distinctive angles. Each stitch should be tacked for fixing.

1 Draw the patterns on the embroidery fabric.

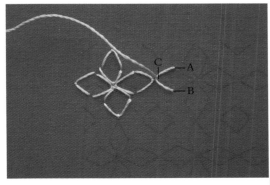

2 Bring out the needle at A to pull out the whole thread. Insert the needle at B and bring it out immediately at C with the thread pressed under the needle. Bring out the needle to pull out the whole thread and tighten it.

3 Insert the needle at D, which is close to C but at the left part of the stitch AB. Bring out the needle to pull out the whole thread and tighten it. This way, the stitch is tacked to complete half of the rhombus.

4 Bring out the needle at E close to A to pull out the whole thread. Insert the needle at F and bring out the needle immediately at G with the thread pressed under the needle.

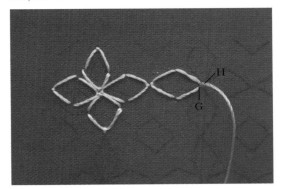

5 Bring out the needle to pull out the whole thread and tighten it. Insert the needle at H, which is close to G but at the outer part of the stitch EF. Bring out the needle to pull out the whole thread and tighten it. This way, the thread is tacked to complete another half of the rhombus.

6 Apply the same method to embroider along the lines already sketched to complete one rhombus after another. Completed.

11. Knot Stitch

It means that each stitch should coil silk threads into small particle-like knots which are densely arrayed in forms. Since each stitch sees a knot, it is the reason for the name of this stitch. It is marked by firmness and durability against wear and tear. All knots are full and even, making embroidered articles appear three dimensional, similar to the effect of objects in relief. The knot stitch was already seen in Chinese embroidery in the Song Dynasty.

Apart from the basic knot stitch, other three kinds of changes will be introduced, i.e. loose knot stitch, knot stitch with a tail, and the Miao ethnicity style knot stitch.

Basic Knot Stitch

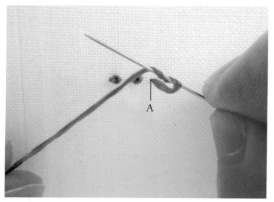

1 Bring out the needle at A to pull out the whole thread. Hold the needle in the right hand. Use the left hand to wind the thread around the needle twice from the inner part to the outer part.

2 Use the left hand to hold the thread taut so that the thread around the needle won't be loose. Then insert the needle at B near A. Pull out the whole thread to complete one knot. Be sure not to use too much strength while pulling out the thread to prevent the knot from falling off. The two knots on the left are completed ones.

Loose Knot Stitch

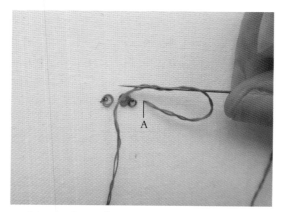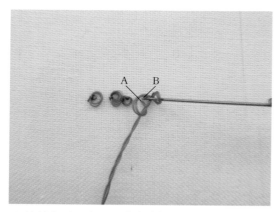

1 Bring out the needle at A to pull out the whole thread. Hold the needle in the right hand; use the left hand to wind the thread on the needle twice from the inner part to the outer part.

2 Hold the thread taut with the left hand to keep the thread loops around the needle. The loops are slightly bigger than those of the basic form of knot stitch. Then insert the needle at B on the right of A.

The Miao Ethnicity Style Knot Stitch

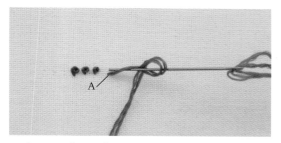

1 Bring out the needle at A to pull out the whole thread. Hold the needle with the right hand. Wind the thread around the needle twice from the inner part to the outer part with the left hand.

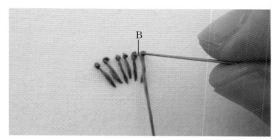

2 Tighten the thread with the left hand to keep the thread around the needle tight. Then insert the needle at B right above A to pull out the whole thread. Be sure the distance between A and B is about 2 mm. Don't use too much strength when pulling the thread. Bring out the whole thread and to complete a knot. Because of the distance between A and B, as well as their position, each knot is like a seed.

Knot Stitch with a Tail

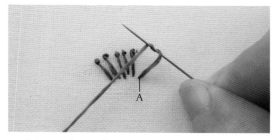

1 Bring out the needle at A to pull out the whole thread. Hold the needle with the right hand; wind the thread with the left hand around the needle twice from the inner part to the outer part.

2 Hold taut the thread with the left hand to keep the thread around the needle tight. Then insert the needle at B right above A and pull out the whole thread. The distance between A and B is the tail of this knot stitch. The distance between A and B can be adjusted according to the actual needs.

Bamboo and Flower Roundel

Based on the pattern on the left, the basic knot stitch is applied to embroider the outer-frame and the stem with brown threads, bamboo leaves with green threads in different shades, and flowers with red, pink, white, and purple threads.

12. Appliqué

Appliqué refers to the cloth cut from other fabrics to be sewn on the fabric as a way of embroidery. Appliqué techniques are simple, marked by patterns in patches. Its unique and attractive style is very popular among people.

The fringe of appliqué patterns is often decorated by gold/silver thread couching stitch, blanket stitch, chain stitch, etc. As a result, the thread-end of the outer fringe of fabrics or coarse parts cannot be seen, hence giving prominence to the pattern.

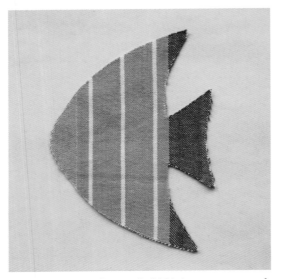

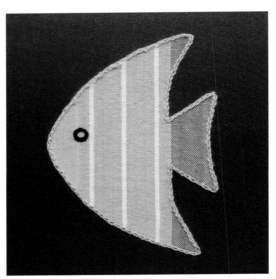

1 Choosing a piece from a colorful fabric to cut a pattern of a tropical fish. Smear the paste or other kind of adhesive on the reverse of the fabric and then stick it onto a piece of green embroidery fabric to be dried.

2 The fringe of the fish is embroidered by the chain stitch to cover the coarse part of the outer fringe. The fish eye is embroidered by chain stitch to complete it.

13. Counted Stitch over Gauze

Already being mature in the Song Dynasty, it is one of the traditional forms of Chinese embroidery. Taking cloth with mesh or gauze as the fabrics, it conducts creation of embroidery regularly according to the meridian and parallel framework of the fabrics.

There are two kinds of counted stitch over gauze. One is marked by embroidered patterns and gauze being left blank. The other one is counted satin stitch over gauze featured by large colorful patches with fully embroidered gauze. Counted stitch over gauze applies vertical, horizontal, and slant stitches of reasonable length. If patterns are a bit complicated on a large area, embroidery can be done in patches alternately after the number of squares is counted to prevent threads from bulging on the gauze and the embroidered surface from being rugged.

The change of silk-thread direction can bring about changeable light reflection, leaving a unique and amazing impression of beauty on people.

Vertical Counted Stitch over Gauze

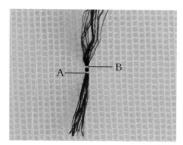

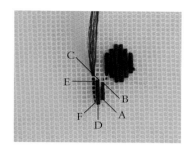

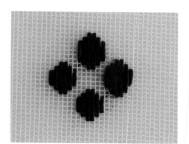

1 Choose a piece of real silk gauze as the fabric (36 small squares within one square inch). Insert the needle at A and bring the needle out at B. AB occupies three small squares. Knotting is not required at the bottom of the embroidery thread, but considerable length should be left behind.

2 Insert the needle again at A to complete the first stitch. Embroidery starts from the right to the left. Bring the needle out at C and insert the needle at D. CD occupies five small squares. Bring the needle out at E and insert the needle at F. EF occupies seven small squares.

3 There are a total of six lines from the right to the left, occupying three small squares, five small squares, seven small squares, seven small squares, five small squares, and three small squares in that order to complete a pattern with an octagonal outer-fringe. Be sure that the unknotted thread-end should be covered in the course of embroidery.

Horizontal Counted Stitch over Gauze

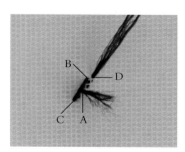

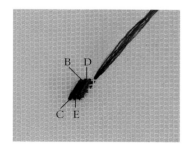

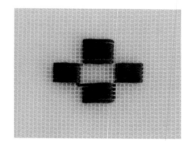

1 Insert the needle at A and bring the needle out at B. Knotting is not required at the bottom of the embroidery thread, but considerable length should be left behind.

2 Count seven squares horizontally. Insert the needle at C to complete the first stitch. DE also occupies seven small squares. Repeat the process and be sure that the unknotted thread-end is covered during the embroidering.

3 Apply the same technique to embroider other rectangles to completion.

Slant Counted Stitch over Gauze

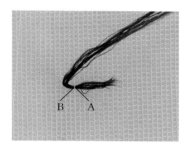

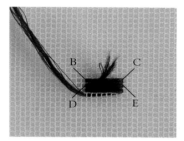

1 Insert the needle at A and make sure the bottom of the embroidery thread is not knotted. Bring the needle out at B and insert the needle at C. BC occupies five small squares. Then bring the needle out at D on the right of B.

2 Insert the needle at E on the right of C. DE also occupies five small squares. The process goes on like this repeatedly. Needle application starts from the left to the right. The number of small squares and the angle for each stitch are the same.

3 Completed. The thread-end exposed outside should be cut off when finished.

Variation of Horizontal Counted Stitch over Gauze

 1 Light blue threads are used to embroider lines of different length horizontally.

 2 Then dark blue threads are used to embroider lines of different length horizontally. Be sure that stitches of dark blue threads are crisscrossed with stitches of light blue threads all over the surface of embroidery, constituting a dual color square.

In the Depth of Birches

This is a piece of work embroidered according to counted stitch over gauze, showing light elegance and uniqueness.

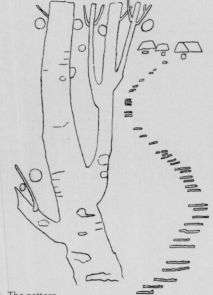

1 The pattern.

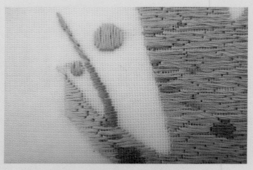

2 Use brown and grass green threads to create the tree trunk and branches by means of the variation of horizontal counted stitch over gauze. Because of the fairly thick trunk, several horizontal stitches are applied with stitches of different length. It happens to show the lines on the barks of the trees. Use grass green threads to create round leaves of different sizes by means of vertical counted stitch over gauze. Apply dark green threads to create small branches by means of slant counted stitch over gauze.

3 Use black threads to create the roof on the left and in the middle, as well as the front of the roof on the right, by means of slant counted stitch over gauze. Use black threads to create the side of the roof on the right by means of vertical counted stitch over gauze. Use brick grey threads to create the window below the roof by means of vertical counted stitch over gauze.

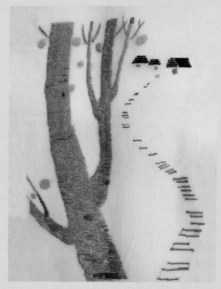

4 Use dark green threads to create the pavement by means of vertical counted stitch over gauze. Completed.

14. Battlement Filling

In the battlement filling, patterns are produced through embroidering threads along a geometric inner frame repeatedly. These patterns produced by battlement filling are obviously featured by a texture of brocade and an effect of bas-relief.

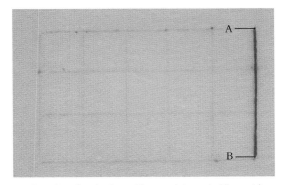

1 First, draw four horizontal lines and six vertical lines with a pencil on the embroidery fabric, forming a geometric pattern consisting of fifteen small squares. Bring out the needle at A and insert at B to make one vertical stitch. Then bring out the needle to pull out the whole thread and tighten it.

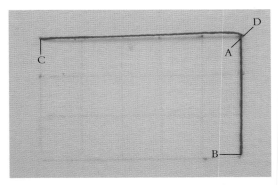

2 Bring out the needle at C and insert at D to make one horizontal stitch. Then bring out the needle to pull out the whole thread and tighten it. AB and CD should all be flatly attached to the embroidery fabric in a straight manner.

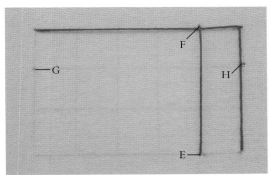

3 Insert the needle at E and bring it out at F to make the second vertical stitch. Then bring out the needle at G and insert at H to make a horizontal stitch. The same procedure follows this to make the second horizontal stitch.

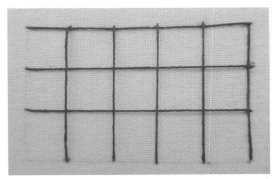

4 With the same method, embroider three horizontal lines and five vertical lines on this geometric pattern with the order of one vertical stitch first and one horizontal stitch second. There is no need to embroider the vertical line on the very left of the geometric pattern and the horizontal line at the very bottom.

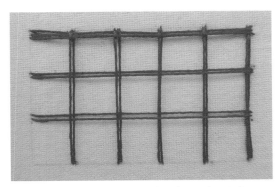

5 The second batch of horizontal stitches and vertical stitches are embroidered following the order and method introduced above. Embroider vertical stitches first.

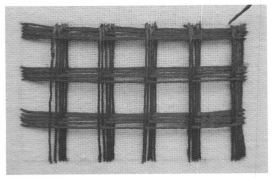

6 Embroider the third batch, the fourth batch, and the fifth batch of horizontal stitches and vertical stitches accordingly.

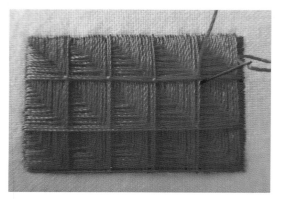

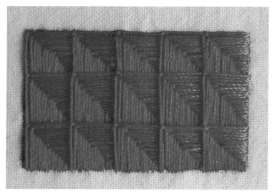

7 With the pattern fully embroidered, apply the most common running stitch to tack a diagonal stitch at the intersection of the squares to prevent the deformation of the pattern due to the sliding of threads.

8 Completed.

15. Weaving Stitch

Use criss-crossed changes to weave plane patterns. Weaving stitch is often applied to embroider the fringe of articles for daily use, making them decorative and resistant to wear and tear. In the following cases, fairly thick cotton threads are chosen for embroidery.

1 First, use green cotton threads to embroider 14 vertical stitches of the same length by means of straight satin stitch. These are the vertical threads with a total width of about 1.5 centimeters. Use yellow cotton threads as horizontal threads and bring two strands of them out at the point very close to the right lower part of vertical threads.

2 From the right to the left, vertical threads go through horizontal threads according to the method of picking up six vertical threads, pressing down two vertical threads, and picking up six vertical threads.

3 Insert the needle into the fabric and then bring it out at the point very close to the fringe near the place where it was inserted. Be sure that the point for inserting the needle and the point for bringing out the needle do not overlap in order to prevent the fall-off when the stitching returns. Then from the left to the right, horizontal threads go through vertical threads according to the method of picking up four vertical threads, pressing down two vertical threads, picking up two vertical threads, pressing down two vertical threads, and picking up four vertical threads.

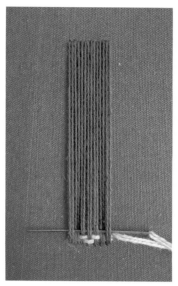

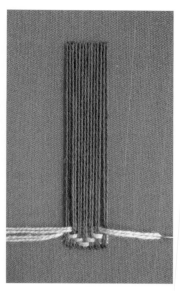

4 Insert the needle into the fabric and then bring it out at the point very close to the fringe near the place where it was inserted. In the wake of it, from the right to the left, horizontal threads go through vertical threads according to the method of picking up two vertical threads, pressing down two vertical threads, picking up six vertical threads, pressing down two vertical threads, and picking up two vertical threads.

5 Insert the needle into the fabric and then bring it out at the point very close to the fringe near the place where it was inserted.

6 In the wake of it, from the left to the right, horizontal threads go through vertical threads according to the method of pressing down two vertical threads, picking up ten vertical threads, and pressing down two vertical threads, hence completing a V-shaped embroidered article.

7 Repeat the method from step one to step five to complete the second V-shaped embroidered article.

8 Apply the same method to complete an upside-down V-shaped embroidered article. Be sure that the order of "picking up" and "pressing down" is just on the contrary to that of the embroidery of a V-shaped article. This way, there will be a rhombus in the middle of the pattern.

9 Repeat the embroidery this way until completion.

16. Cross Stitch

Cross stitch is able to create many very small crosses to constitute various patterns. Simple as they seem to be, they present themselves in different forms. Cross stitch is popular and extensively used in all parts of China.

It is true that Chinese cross stitch is the same as Western cross stitch in terms of needlework. However, Western cross stitch has to rely on the squares on the embroidery fabrics to conduct embroidery. In contrast, Chinese cross stitch relies completely on a horizontal and vertical array, which is neat, detailed, and attractive, free from the restriction of squares on the embroidery fabrics.

Chinese cross stitch is divided into basic cross stitch, half cross stitch, quarter cross stitch, and herringbone cross stitch. First, attention should be paid to the coordination between eyes and the needle. The left side should be embroidered first before it comes to the right side, so as not to block the eyesight.

Basic Cross Stitch

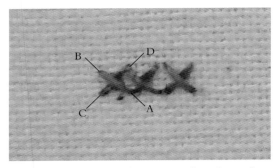

Bring the needle out at A and insert at B. Pull out the needle to bring out the whole thread and tightened. Bring the needle out at C and insert at D. Pull out the needle to bring out the whole thread and tighten to complete the first cross. Apply the same method to create the other crosses.

Half Cross Stitch

Bring the needle out at A and insert at B. Pull out the needle to bring out the whole thread and tighten to complete. Bring the needle out at C and insert at D, close to A. AB and CD are respectively seen at the cross of 1/4. Apply the same method to create the pattern as you desire.

Quarter Cross Stitch

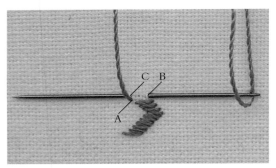

Bring the needle out at A. Pull out the needle to bring out the whole thread. Insert the needle at B and bring the needle out immediately at C, close to A. Keep A and B on a par. Apply the same method to bring about the pattern as you desire.

Herringbone Cross Stitch

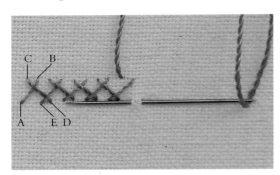

Bring the needle out at A with the whole thread brought out. Insert the needle at B and immediately bring the needle out at C with the whole thread brought out. Insert the needle at D and immediately bring the needle out at E with the whole thread brought out. Apply the same method to bring about the pattern as you desire.

The Horse and the War-Chariot

The horse and the war-chariot were embroidered by cross stitch according to the design.

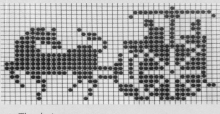

1 The design.

2 Each cross is in a neat array according to the design. The point at which the needle was brought out and inserted can be on a par in all directions, hence leading to neat crosses.

17. Sparse Stitch

Both ends of the stitch of sparse stitch are connected and criss-crossed, slightly showing the fabric.

There are two kinds of sparse stitch, i.e. vertical sparse stitch and horizontal sparse stitch. It is quite appropriate to use vertical sparse stitch to depict mountains in the distance, while horizontal sparse stitch is mostly applied to embroider clouds, water-ripples, background, and bamboo curtains. Threads used for sparse stitch are often marked by different thickness and colors of different shades, being able to reveal substance within vacancy.

Horizontal Sparse Stitch

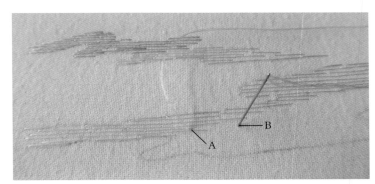

1 First, draw the water-ripple outline on the embroidery fabric. Horizontal sparse stitch, when used in embroidery, goes from the left to the right. Just like vertical sparse stitch, when used in embroidery, both ends of the stitches of horizontal sparse stitch should be connected. Bring the needle out at A and insert at B. A is the end of the preceding stitch.

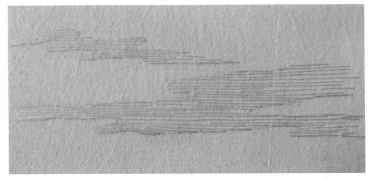

2 It is completed. The space between the upper stitches and the lower stitches of horizontal sparse stitch is also quite sparse with different lengths. Silk threads of different shades are applied, as if clouds in the sky are reflected on the water surface.

Vertical Sparse Stitch

1 Use a pencil to draw a wave-shaped line on the fabric, representing the outline of mountains in the distance. Vertical sparse stitch, when used in embroidery, goes from the top to the bottom. Bring the needle out at A and insert at B with the needle pulled out and the whole thread brought out to complete the first stitch. Then bring the needle out at C and insert at D. Be sure that the length of the stitch of AB and CD is different.

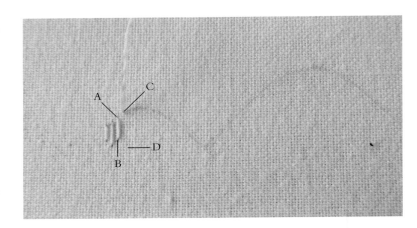

2 Apply the same method to complete the embroidery of the first band in which the length of the stitch changes and its array is quite sparse.

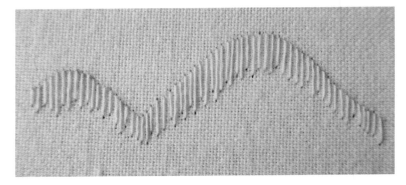

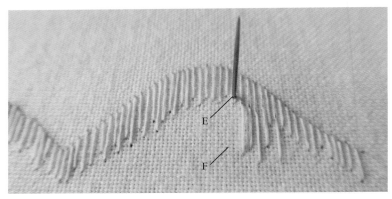

3 For the embroidery of the second band, the head of the stitches should be connected with the end of the stitches of the first band. Bring the needle out at E (E is at the end of the stitch of the preceding band) and insert at F.

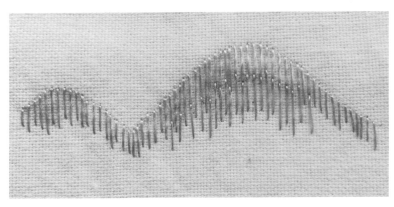

4 There should also be changes in the length of the stitches of the second band with quite sparse array. Completed.

18. Fishbone Stitch

Such needlework gets its name from the fact that its products look like fishbone. The needlework can be divided into basic fishbone stitch, open fishbone stitch, and raised fishbone stitch.

Basic Fishbone Stitch

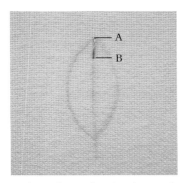

1 Insert the needle at A at the top of the leaf and bring out at B with the needle pulled out. Bring out the whole thread and tighten.

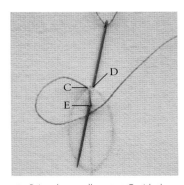

2 Bring the needle out at C with the whole thread brought out and tighten. Then insert the needle at D and bring out at E. Pull out the thread, with the thread beneath needle.

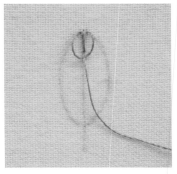

3 With the whole thread brought out, there will be a loop formed and tightened.

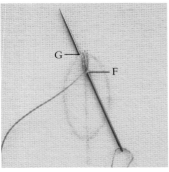

4 Insert the needle at F and bring out at G, with the whole thread brought out and tightened.

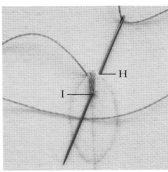

5 Insert the needle at H and bring out at I. The thread is beneath the needle after the latter is pulled out with the whole thread brought out and tightened.

6 Apply the same method to go on with the embroidery. Be sure that the distance between stitches should be short so as to produce an effect of firmness and density.

7 Completed.

Fresh Greenery
Try to use a pencil to draw a leaf-sketch on the embroidery fabric. Then use basic fishbone stitch and green silk threads to create the scene of spring as follows.

Open Fishbone Stitch

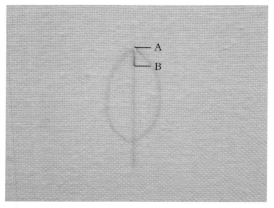

1 Bring the needle out at A at the top of the leaf and insert at B with the whole thread brought out and tightened.

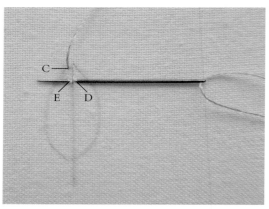

2 Bring the needle out at C, insert at D, and bring the needle out at E with the whole thread brought out and tightened.

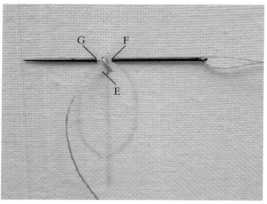

3 Insert the needle at F and bring the needle out at G with the whole thread brought out and tightened.

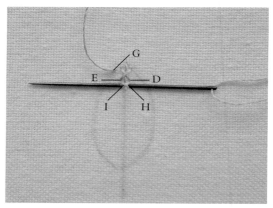

4 Insert the needle at H and bring out at I with the whole thread brought out and tightened. Make sure that H and I are right below D and E respectively at an interval of three to four stitches.

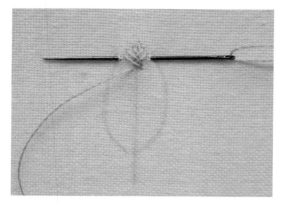

5 Apply the same method to go on with the embroidery. Please note that the inclining stitches become longer and longer along with the change of the leaf-outline. However, the angle remains unchanged and space between stitches is kept balanced.

6 Moreover, stitches should all reach the verge via the central line. Attention should also be paid to keeping an even distance between inclining stitches in a quite sparse array. Completed.

Raised Fishbone Stitch

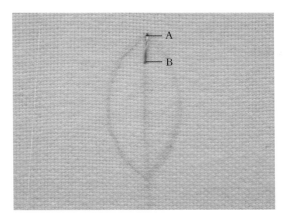

1 Bring the needle out at A at the top of the leaf and insert at B with the whole thread brought out and tightened.

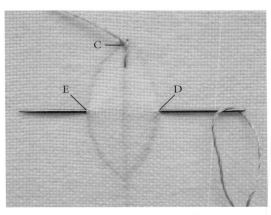

2 Bring the needle out at C, insert at D, and bring out at E. Be sure that D and E are located at the widest part of the leaf blade.

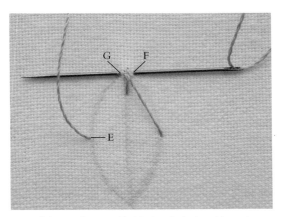

3 Pull the needle out at E with the whole thread brought out and tightened. Then insert the needle at F and bring out at G on a par with F with the needle pulled out. Bring out the whole thread and tighten.

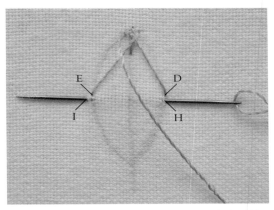

4 Insert the needle at H and bring out at I. H and I should be located right below D and E respectively.

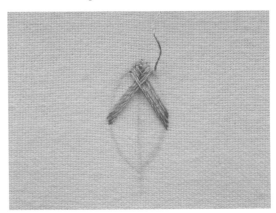

5 Apply the same method to handle embroidery in a cross way along the leaf-outline, i.e. from the upper part of the left to the lower part of the right and from the upper part of the right to the lower part of the left.

6 Completed.

FIG. 47 *Flowers*

The entwined flowers on this embroidered article are often seen on embroidered articles for daily use. The branches are mainly embroidered by shaded satin stitch and stem stitch. Along with the change of curving branches, even plain flowers also appear charming and spirited.

19. Slanted Satin Stitch

Embroidery is done by the slanted satin stitch in slanted short lines seemingly encircling the pattern. The needle is brought out from one side and inserted on the other side, always keeping in the same direction. The slanted satin stitch can change the angle of embroidery threads flexibly to control the direction of embroidery. It is usually applied to create small leaves, stems and branches and embroidery threads are generally of a single color.

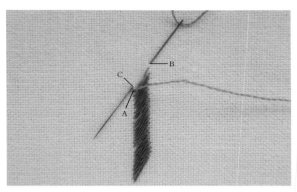

Bring the needle out at A. Insert the needle at B and immediately bring the needle out at C. AB is a stitch of the slanted satin stitch. The angle of slanted AB stitch is usually smaller than or equal to 45°. The process goes like this repeatedly according to the pattern on the embroidery fabric until the embroidery is completed.

Orchid

This piece of work was completed by the slanted satin stitch. According to the design, green silk threads were applied to create orchid leaves, while yellowish green silk threads were used to create orchid flowers.

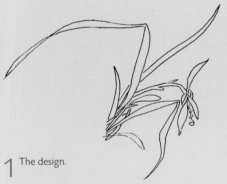

1 The design.

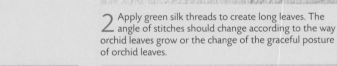

2 Apply green silk threads to create long leaves. The angle of stitches should change according to the way orchid leaves grow or the change of the graceful posture of orchid leaves.

3 Apply yellowish green silk threads to create the orchid flowers. The angle of slanted stitches should change according to the posture of hanging orchid flowers.

4 Completed.

20. Shaded Satin Stitch

Shaded satin stitch started in the Tang Dynasty and became quite mature in the Song Dynasty. No stitch-trace can be found in its application. It is good at expressing the integration of colors of different shades and changes, possessing the effect of shaded dyeing in Chinese paintings.

There are two kinds, i.e. regular shaded satin stitch and long and short shaded satin stitch. Stitches of regular shaded satin stitch are quite neat. Each band of threads is separated from the other, with the color becoming gradually soft and the embroidery surface smooth. Stitches of long and short shaded satin stitch are reasonably scattered, with very natural transition of the color.

Regular Shaded Satin Stitch

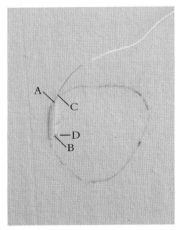

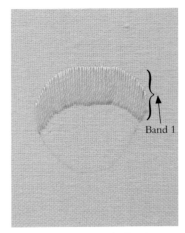

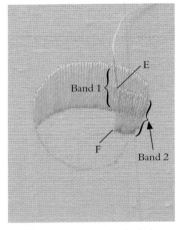

1 Now, let's embroider a piece of petal from the top to the bottom in five bands. The color of threads should also be divided into five kinds. Bring the needle out at A and insert at B, bringing out the whole thread and tightening it to complete the first stitch. Then bring the needle out at C and insert at D.

2 Apply the same method to the embroidery from the left to the right to complete the first band. Be sure that the length of the stitch is about 1 to 2 centimeters. The stitches should be kept vertical in a neat array.

3 Choose some threads of a darker color to embroider the second band. Bring the needle out at E and insert at F. E lies at the vertical middle point of the first-band stitches as well as between the left stitch and the right stitch.

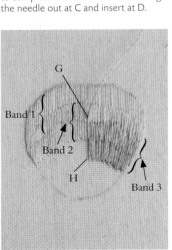

4 With the second band completed, embroidery of the third band starts with some of the threads of the darker color used. Bring the needle out at G and insert at H. G lies at the mid-point between the upper stitch and the lower stitch of the second band, as well as between the left stitch and the right stitch. This point is situated exactly at a place one millimeter above the end of the first-band stitches. In other words, the head of the third-band stitches is connected with the end of the first-band stitches.

5 Apply the same method to embroider the fourth band and the fifth band. Completed.

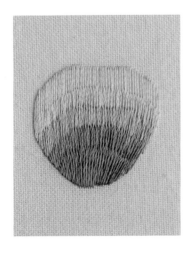

Long and Short Shaded Satin Stitch

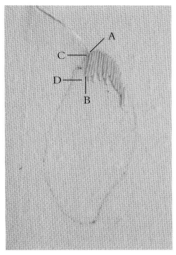

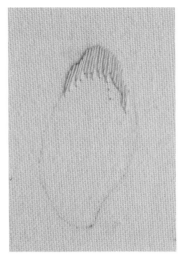

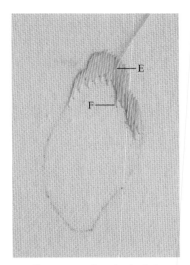

1 Now, let's embroider a piece of petal by means of long and short shaded satin stitch, with the petal being embroidered from the top to the bottom in five bands. First, draw the petal outline with a pencil before the first band is embroidered. Bring the needle out at A and insert at B with the whole thread brought out and tightened, leading to the completion of a stitch. Then bring the needle out at C and insert at D, from the right to the left in that order.

2 Be sure that all points at which the needle is brought out are on the outline. The stitch should be no longer than one centimeter, the point into which the needle is inserted is not regular, and the stitches are marked by different lengths. In the picture is the effect of the first-band stitches after completion.

3 Choose some threads of a darker color to embroider the second band. Bring the needle out at E and insert at F. E lies between the left stitch and the right stitch of the first band. The vertical mid-point of the first-band stitches is even higher, with the highest point being at a place of 70% or 80% of the stitch. The second-band stitches are of the same lengths, however, due to different heights of the points at which the needle is brought out and inserted, the second-band stitches turn out to be unbalanced.

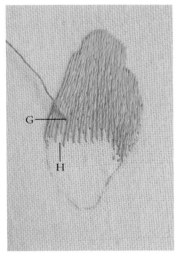

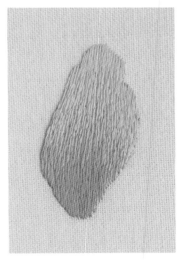

4 Repeat the method of the second band to complete the third band. This shows the effect after completion. The heads of third-band stitches are connected with the ends of first-band stitches.

5 Please refer to the method for embroidering the second band to embroider the third and the left bands of long and short shaded satin stitch.

6 Apply the same method to embroider the fourth band and the fifth band. It is completed. The color transition of long and short shaded satin stitch is more natural and tender than that of regular shaded satin stitch, without abrupt traces.

21. Star Stitch

It is named so because it radiates outward from the center. This stitch is suitable for embroidering pine needles, water weeds, as well as the stamens of plum blossoms and peach flowers, etc.

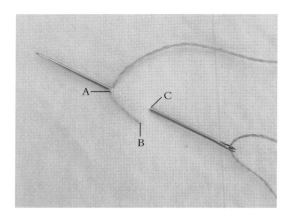

1 With A as the center, bring out the needle at A, insert it at B and then immediately bring it out at A. Bring out the needle and pull out the whole thread. Tighten the thread. The first stitch is completed. Then insert the needle at C and immediately bring it out at A. Pull out the whole thread and tighten it. The second stitch is completed.

2 Each stitch is centered around A, creating a radiating pattern. Be sure that the stitch length is the same with the same angle at every interval.

3 An example of star stitch.

Pine Needles
Following the pattern on the left, use green threads of different shades to embroider pine needles.

22. Twining Thread Couching Stitch

Mastery of this technique requires the mastery of "twining threads" first. Hard threads should be chosen as "core threads" (core threads can also be starched to increase their hardness). Core threads are then twined with colored fine threads, hence leading to "twining threads." Horsetail hair threads and peacock feather threads introduced in Chapter Two are two kinds of "twining threads" made from different "core threads."

To be specific, patterns are outlined by twining threads to be stuck with tacking threads for fixation. Firm colorful sewing threads are used as tacking threads, with the color being the same as that of twining threads. However, in the following explanation, two colors are used to differentiate twining threads from tacking threads.

Twining thread couching stitch is frequently seen in the Bijie area in Guizhou Province, China. It is also occasionally used in Chaozhou Embroidery and the other schools of embroidery. This is quite the special embroidery for decoration.

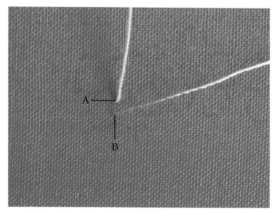

1 A light blue twining thread goes through the needle eye with the needle brought out at A. Bring the yellow tacking thread out at B.

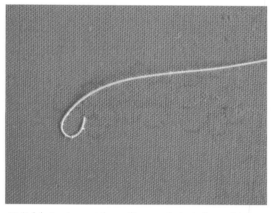

2 While turning out the outline you desire to have with the twining thread, you can fix the twining thread with the tacking thread.

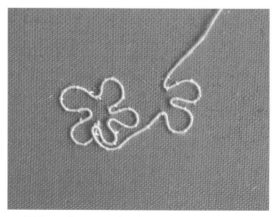

3 With one flower completed, you can move the twining thread to the location of the next flower for embroidery using the same method.

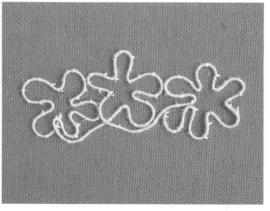

4 After this piece is done, you can insert the twining thread to bring it to the reverse of the embroidery fabric to be knotted and cut. Completed.

23. Coiling Stitch

A thick needle and a fine needle should be used for it at the same time. The big-eye needle strung with a thick thread encircles the small-eye needle to form a thick coil, while the small-eye needle strung with a fine thread tacks the thick coil. This process goes on repeatedly to embroider patterns. The thick thread (circling thread) and the fine thread (tacking thread) can be of the same color or different colors.

Articles for daily use embroidered by coiling stitch are exquisite and solid. They are not vulnerable to damage or even suffer from some wear and tear. Moreover, thanks to the application of two kinds of threads, colors are rich and the effect of works is more varied.

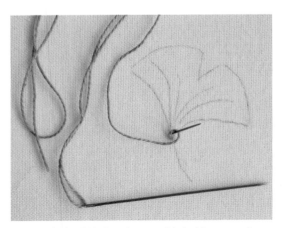

1 Prepare two needles of embroidery. The big-eye needle is strung with a thick thread of the green color. The small-eye needle is strung with a yellow fine thread.

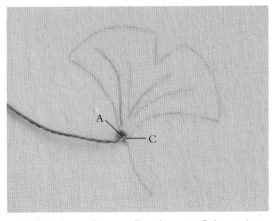

2 Draw the pattern on the embroidery fabric. Proceed from the root of the ginkgo leaf to embroider the outline of the leaf clockwise before embroidering the stem. Bring the big-eye needle out at A to pull out the whole thread. Then bring the small-eye needle out at B with half of the needle exposed. Be sure that B is also on the outline.

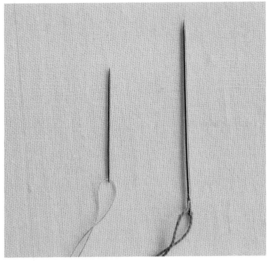

3 Encircle the thick thread strung with the big-eye needle clockwise around the small-eye needle.

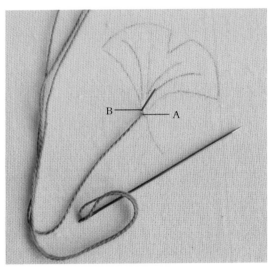

4 Pull out the small-eye needle and insert at C close to A to tack the thick thread, completing the first small circle.

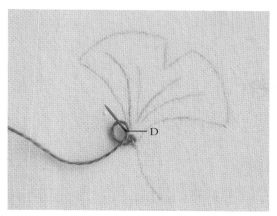

5 Bring the small-eye needle out at D in the wake of the needle-trace forward with half of the needle exposed. Encircle the thick thread around the small-eye needle clockwise.

6 While pulling out the small-eye needle to bring out the fine thread, use your left hand to press down the thick coil gently to prevent the thick coil from being deformed when the small-eye needle is being pulled out.

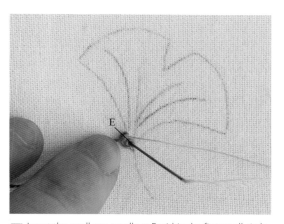

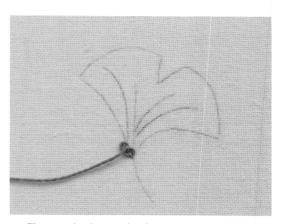

7 Insert the small-eye needle at E within the first small circle to tack the second small coil.

8 The second coil is completed.

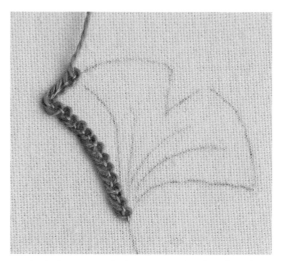

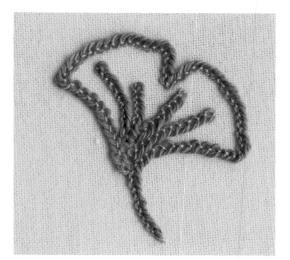

9 Apply the same method to repeat embroidery along the outline of the sketch.

10 Completed.

24. Bullion Knot

It is frequently applied in Chinese embroidery and Western embroidery. There are two kinds, i.e. straight bullion knot and circle bullion knot. Works produced by bullion knot are marked by full patterns and a strong sense of three dimensions. Bullion knots of good quality are well proportioned, without redundant and loose knots of irregular shapes.

Straight Bullion Knot

1 Draw the pattern on the embroidery fabric. Each short arc line is a straight bullion knot.

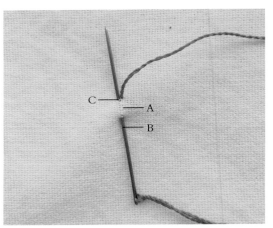

2 Bring the needle out at A to pull out the whole thread. Insert the needle at B and bring the needle out at C at once, but the needle should not be pulled out. Be sure that C is near A. B and C are respectively the head and the end of a straight bullion knot.

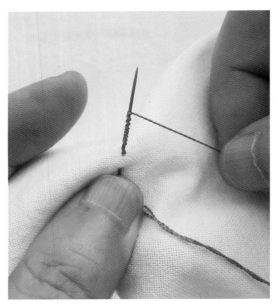

3 Use the left hand to hold the embroidery fabric, with the thumb holding the needle-tail. Use the right hand to twist the thread around the needle for about ten times.

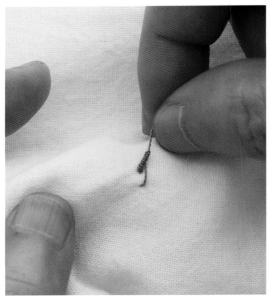

4 Pull out the needle and tighten the thread.

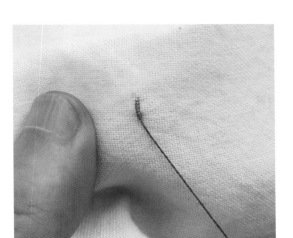

5 Bring the thread toward yourself to complete the first straight bullion knot, making it flat and smooth on the fabric.

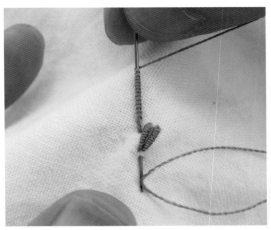

6 Repeat the above mentioned steps for embroidery according to the pattern.

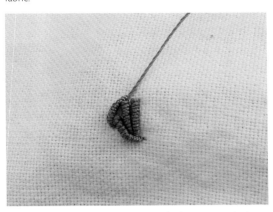

7 Several knots form the petals. Apply the same method to complete the pattern.

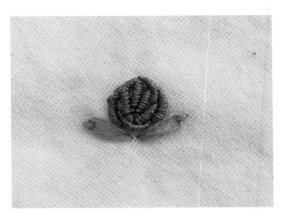

8 With the straight bullion knots completed, apply the chain stitch to create two green leaves as ornaments.

Circle Bullion Knot

1 Draw the pattern on the embroidery fabric.

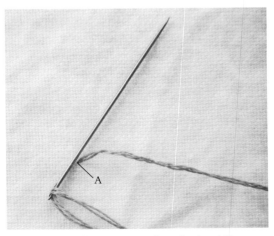

2 Bring the needle out at A to pull out the thread. Then place the needle on the left of A.

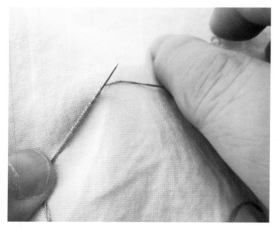

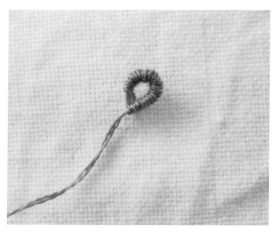

3 Use the left hand to hold the embroidery fabric with the thumb holding the needle-tail. Use the right hand to twist the thread around the needle for about twenty-two times.

4 Draw out the needle towards yourself to tighten the thread, making it a round shape.

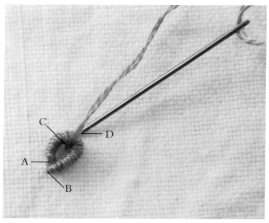

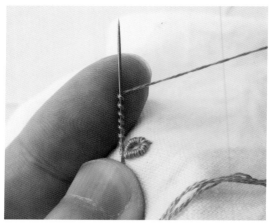

5 Insert the needle into embroidery fabric at B near A. Then bring the needle out at C, which is inside the upper part within the round petal. Insert the needle at D with one stitch for fixation to complete the first circle bullion knot.

6 Apply the same method to continue with the embroidery.

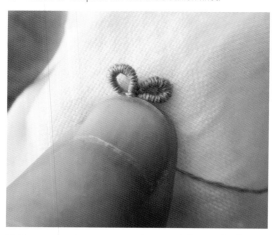

7 Be sure that the more you twist around the needle, the bigger the round shape is.

8 With the petals embroidered, use chain stitch to create three green leaves as ornaments.

25. Free Cross Stitch

It is a kind of needlework overlapped by long lines and short lines, able to achieve the effect of blending, feathering, and layering of color, making the embroidered article look like an oil painting. Free cross stitch consists of three forms, i.e. small free cross stitch, big free cross stitch, and the hash tag mark free cross stitch.

Bring out the needle at A and insert it at B. Pull out the whole thread tightly. Then bring out the needle at C and insert it at D. Cross the stitch AB with stitch CD. Repeat and continue to cross stitches until completion.

    Be sure that the stitch length of the small free cross stitch is shorter than 1 cm and that the cross-angle between stitches is at an acute angle.

Small Free Cross Stitch

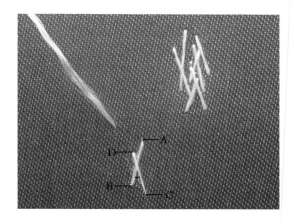

Big Free Cross Stitch

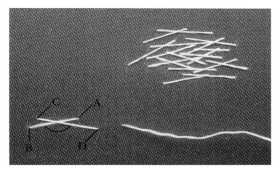

Bring out the needle at A and insert it at B. Pull out the whole thread tightly. Then bring out the needle at C and insert it at D. Cross the stitch AB with stitch CD. Repeat and continue to cross stitches until completion.

    Be sure that the stitch length of the big free cross stitch should be longer than 1 cm and that the cross-angle between stitches should be a blunt angle that is more at random. With this stitch used for embroidery, it would be appropriate to avoid vertical and horizontal lines.

Hash Tag Mark Free Cross Stitch

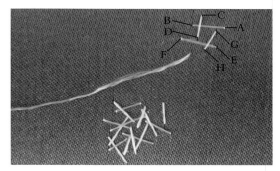

Bring the needle out at A and insert at B. Bring out the needle and pull out the whole thread. Tighten the thread. The same way is applied to the other three stitches of CD, EF, and GH to cross irregular overlapping hash tag mark-shaped patterns.

Daisies

Free cross stitch for different parts:

    Petals: small free cross stitch

    Green leaves: small free cross stitch

    Stamens: hash tag mark free cross stitch

CHAPTER FOUR
EMBROIDERY PROJECTS FOR DAILY USE

With the basic needlework acquired, you can apply it in daily life. This chapter will introduce nineteen kinds of embroidery of daily life, e.g. one corner of a napkin is embroidered with a pierced chrysanthemum, a white skirt is embroidered with dandelion and wild chrysanthemum patterns, a handbag is embroidered with butterfly and flower patterns, etc. Colorful embroidered articles of daily life can add depth to your environment.

With colorful threads applied to embroidery fabric of different colors, you can experience the appeal of the needle and threads as well as a feeling of tranquility. There is no doubt that you will feel immensely fulfilled after the embroidery is completed. Let's embark on the beautiful journey of embroidery together!

In this chapter, except where indicated, all articles are embroidered by half of a piece of silk thread, i.e. eight strands of silk thread.

FIG. 48   Embroidery of the ethnic minorities in China
Patterns and needlework of embroidery of the ethnic minorities in China are marked by the appeal of remote antiquity. The cloth is ingeniously seamed with another cloth while the needlework is harmoniously integrated with threads. On the condition that attractiveness is kept, durability as the most fundamental thing is always in the minds of embroiderers. Therefore, the embroiderer would spare no time and cost to deal with each embroidered article for daily use.

1. Pottery Jar of Geometric Patterns

Battlement filling is fully applied to this project. Geometric patterns on different parts are overlapped to produce effects of color painting and coarse texture on the jar. This pattern could be used as decoration in any place. It could also be put into a frame as a decorative picture.

This pottery jar of geometric patterns has three parts, i.e. its middle part is crisscrossed by slanted lines, its lower part consists of vertical and horizontal lines, and its upper part is the most complex since there are horizontal lines and crisscrossed slanted lines.

The completion of a bigger pattern requires the enlargement of the pattern and the increase of the number of stitches in each batch of battlement filling. Or you can change the color of embroidery threads to see different effects.

The Size Suggested
6 × 5 cm

You Will Need
Embroidery needle: 9#
Embroidery fabric: white cotton cloth
Embroidery threads:
  The jar-body: grey silk threads and dark red silk threads
  The cover: brown silk threads
  The jar-bottom: brown silk threads

Stitch Diagram
■ ■ ■ Battlement filling (page 67)

Stitch Guide

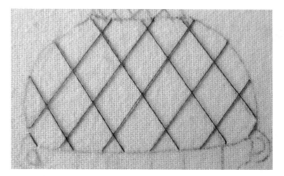

1 Embroider the body of the jar first. Embroider with slanted lines from the right to the left using grey silk threads. Then embroider slanted lines from the left to the right to complete the first-batch stitches.

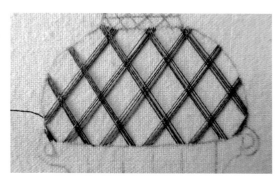

2 The process goes on like this repeatedly. Each batch should be embroidered in order in a neat array.

3 Sixteen batches of grey stitches are needed for the body of the jar. Be sure that the location of fine and dark red stitches should be set aside. With the same method, change grey silk threads into dark red silk threads for embroidery. It goes on repeatedly from the right to the left first and then from the left to the right. About five batches of dark red stitches are required.

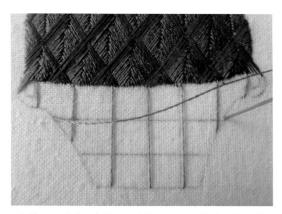

4 Change dark red silk threads into brown silk threads, with slanted lines embroidered from the right to the left first, and horizontal lines embroidered from the top to the bottom.

5 About fifteen vertical stitches and twenty horizontal stitches are needed for each square on the bottom of the jar to complete its embroidery.

6 The cover is embroidered with brown silk threads, with horizontal stitches embroidered from the top to the bottom first, and slanted stitches embroidered from the left to the right. The process goes on like this repeatedly. About seven horizontal stitches and four slanted stitches are needed for each layer.

2. Pierced Chrysanthemum Napkin

A plain white and simple napkin, despite the lack of some novelty, can immediately become elegant when one of its corners is embroidered with one or two flowers.

In the following case, we have chosen chrysanthemum patterns. In ancient China, chrysanthemums were very popular among scholars who eulogized them so much in poetry because of their proud blossom in defiance of the autumn cold. Tao Yuanming, a poet in the Eastern Jin Dynasty (about 365–427), wrote this famous verse "Picking chrysanthemums at the foot of eastern bamboo fence while leisurely seeing the southern mountain," which advise staying far away from worldly noise as well as seeking no fame and gain.

The Size Suggested
45 × 45 cm

You Will Need
Embroidery needle: 9#
Embroidery fabric: white cotton cloth
Embroidery thread: white cotton threads

Stitch Diagram
■ Slanted satin stitch (page 77)
■ Blanket stitch (page 47)

Stitch Guide

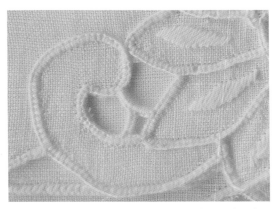

1 Apply white cotton threads and slanted satin stitch to embroider rice-shaped patterns inside the petal. Be sure that the petal has two layers, with the outer layer extending outward and the inner layer curling inward. Then use white cotton threads and blanket stitch to embroider the outer fringe of the petal.

2 Use white cotton threads and blanket stitch to embroider scrolling-leaf patterns at both ends of the petal. Then cut off the exposed fabric between the scrolling-leaf patterns and the petal.

3 Use white cotton threads and blanket stitch to embroider the stamens. Then cut off the exposed fabric amidst the stamens.

4 Use white cotton threads and blanket stitch to embroider leaves. Then cut off the exposed fabric amidst the leaves.

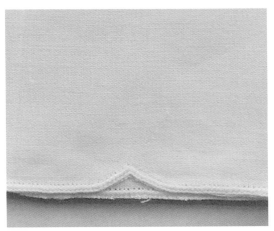

5 Use white cotton threads and blanket stitch to embroider the outer fringe of the napkin. Then cut off the exposed fabric from the parts embroidered with blanket stitch.

6 Completed.

3. Handkerchief with Flower Patterns

One of the corners of a plain color handkerchief is embroidered with an exquisite flower in purple, pink, and green colors. This handkerchief gives one a sense of peace and tranquility. It is suitable to be used for yourself or to be given as a gift.

The Size Suggested
27 × 27 cm

You Will Need
Embroidery needle: 9#
Embroidery fabric: white plain crepe satin
Embroidery threads:
    The leaf: silk threads of green shades
    The stem: silk threads of green shades
    The calyx: purple silk threads
    The petal: silk threads of pink shades

Stitch Diagram
◻◼ Long and short shaded satin stitch (page 79)
◼ Slanted satin stitch (page 77)
◼ Stem stitch (page 51)

Stitch Guide

1 Apply silk threads of green shades and long and short shaded satin stitch to embroider leaves. Then use dark green silk threads and stem stitch to embroider leaf veins amidst leaves.

2 Use dark green silk threads and slanted satin stitch to embroider stems.

3 Use purple silk threads and slanted satin stitch to embroider the calyx. Apply silk threads of pink shades and long and short shaded satin stitch to embroider petals.

4 Sew the rough fringes of the handkerchief all around. Iron the handkerchief flat under appropriate temperature.

4. Powder Compact Mirror with Rose Patterns

Does a metal compact powder mirror feel ice cold? Try to decorate it with embroidery. Embroidery fabric made of cotton and linen is warm, making such a mirror even softer when you feel it. Pink rose patterns enjoy the texture of softness and gorgeousness. Embroidery makes your compact powder mirror unique.

The Size Suggested
6.5 cm in diameter

You Will Need
Embroidery needle: 9#
Embroidery fabric: light purple cotton linen cloth
Embroidery threads:
    The flower: cotton threads of peach-red shades
    The stem: yellow cotton threads
    The leaf: green cotton threads

Stitch Diagram
▮ Closed chain stitch (page 43)
▮ Running stitch (page 42)
▮ ▮ Straight bullion knot (page 84)
▮ Circle bullion knot (page 85)

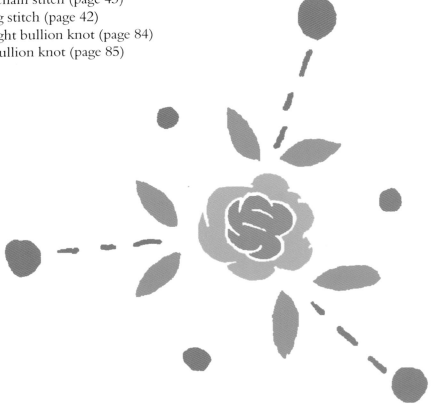

Stitch Guide

1 Apply green cotton threads and closed chain stitch to embroider three pairs of leaves.

2 Apply four strands of yellow cotton threads and running stitch to embroider three stems, each with three stitches of different lengths.

3 Use four strands of peach-red cotton threads and straight bullion knot to embroider the rose in the center of the diagram. There are three layers embroidered from the inner part to the outer part. The color of threads gradually becomes lighter and lighter. In the innermost layer, each bullion knot loops six times. In the second layer, each bullion knot loops eight times. In the outermost layer, each bullion knot loops ten times.

4 Apply four strands of peach-red cotton threads and circle bullion knots to embroider the big flower outside the stem. Apply peach-red cotton threads and circle bullion knots to embroider small flowers amidst stems.

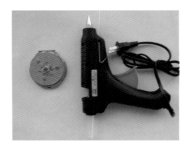

5 Completed. With the rose as the center, cut the embroidery fabric into a round shape of 7.5 cm in diameter.

6 Prepare a round card of 6.5 cm in diameter and glue the embroidered article onto the card.

7 The surface of the powder compact mirror is glued with the embroidered article onto the card with a hot glue gun. Completed.

5. Name-Card Case Embroidered with a Pattern of Dual *Ruyi*

As one of the traditional arts and crafts in China, *ruyi* consists of a fine and long handle as well as a head of cloud pattern. It stands for auspiciousness. The following dual-headed *ruyi* signifies praying for double the good luck.

The Size Suggested
8.6 × 4.8 cm

You Will Need
Embroidery needle: 9# long
Embroidery fabric: black cotton cloth
Embroidery threads:
  The inner part of *ruyi* handle: rust-red sewing threads
  The outline of *ruyi* handle: silver threads and blue sewing threads
  Cloud patterns of *ruyi* head: silver threads, orange sewing threads, and yellow sewing threads
  Leaf blades: green sewing threads

Stitch Diagram
■ Closed chain stitch (page 43)
◻ ◼ ◼ Silver thread couching stitch (page 58)
■ Slanted satin stitch (page 77)

Stitch Guide

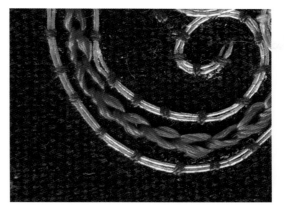

1 Use rust-red threads and closed chain stitch to embroider the inner part of the *ruyi* handle. Then use two strands of silver threads and silver thread couching stitch to finish the outline of the *ruyi* handle. At the same time, use blue sewing threads to tack two strands of silver threads.

2 Use two strands of silver threads and silver thread couching stitch to finish the four cloud patterns on the *ruyi* head. Use orange sewing threads to tack the two strands of silver threads simultaneously to complete the three cloud patterns on the outer flank. Use yellow sewing threads to tack the two strands of silver threads at the same time to complete the cloud pattern on the inner flank.

3 Apply green sewing threads and slanted satin stitch to embroider four leaves.

4 Completed. With the embroidered article as the center, cut the embroidery fabric into the size of 9.6 × 5.8 cm.

5 Prepare a card of 8.6 × 4.8 cm and glue the embroidered surface onto the card.

6 Glue the outer cover of the name card case with the embroidery article by means of a hot glue gun. Completed.

6. Small Melons with Trailing Stems and Branches

Small melons with trailing stems and branches are a traditional auspicious pattern in China. In the initial period of its growth, the melon is very small but its trailing stems and branches continue to grow, representing a bountiful harvest and lots of children.

   Two small yellow melons in the pattern look sweet and delicious as they are coupled with leaves of green and white squares. Embroidery threads in contrast with colors of the embroidery fabric make this article more lively. This embroidered pattern can be used to decorate child garments and book bags.

The Size Suggested
12 × 7 cm

You Will Need
Embroidery needle: 9#
Embroidery fabric: white cotton cloth
Appliqué:
The melon: yellow cotton cloth
Leaves: white-green plaid cotton cloth
The footstalk of the melon: orange-red cotton cloth
Embroidery threads:
   Melon veins: green plait-weaving threads (see page 38) and green sewing threads
   The footstalk of the melon: earth yellow cotton threads
   Melon vines: green cotton threads
   Leaf veins: rust-red cotton threads
   Leaf-outline: green cotton threads

Stitch Diagram
■ Simple couching stitch (refer to gold/silver thread couching stitch on page 58)
■ ■ ■ Appliqué (page 64)
■ ■ Running stitch (page 42)
■ Stem stitch (page 51)

Stitch Guide

1 Use carbon paper to transfer melon patterns onto the yellow cotton cloth. Cut off the patterns.

2 Use carbon paper to transfer melon-leaf patterns onto the white-green plaid cotton cloth. Cut off the patterns.

3 Glue the yellow melon patterns onto the white cotton cloth. Use simple couching stitch to tack green plait-weaving threads onto the melon veins.

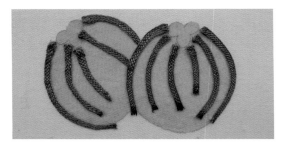

4 Each melon vein should be couched a bit longer to be covered by the leaves later.

5 Leaves are added to the yellow melons. Then cut off the orange red cotton cloth into two three-leaf patterns to add as footstalks. Draw fine melon stems and branches on both sides of the melon according to the design.

6 Use earth-yellow cotton threads and running stitch to embroider melon footstalks.

7 Apply green cotton threads and stem stitch to embroider fine melon vines.

8 Use rust-red cotton threads and stem stitch to embroider stems. Apply green cotton threads and running stitch to embroider the leaf-fringes.

7. Bookmark Bag with Calabash Pattern

The calabash in a nice shape sounds like "happiness and wealth" in Chinese. It is a traditional pattern popular among common folks in China, expressing the longing of people for happy lives. This embroidered article can be used as a bookmark bag and a mobile phone bag, etc., enjoying extensive uses.

The Size Suggested
13 × 7 cm

You Will Need
Embroidery needle: 9#
Embroidery fabric: two piece of pale pinkish grey cotton cloth, 13 × 7 cm
Embroidery threads:
    The calabash: blue twining threads and blue sewing threads
    Ornaments: red and blue beads and white sewing threads

Stitch Diagram
■ Twining thread couching stitch (page 81)
■ ▨ Bead work (page 52)

Stitch Guide

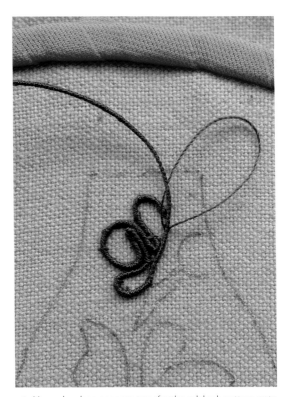

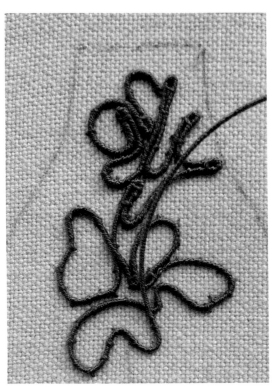

1 Use red carbon paper to transfer the calabash pattern onto the cotton cloth. Bring the blue twining threads out of the embroidery fabric first. Then embroidery proceeds with blue sewing threads and twining thread couching stitch according to the direction of the patterns.

2 Embroidery goes with tacking together and there should be no cut-off along the way.

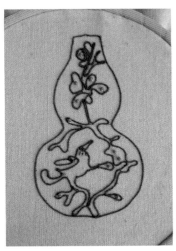

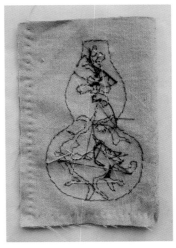

3 With the twining thread couching stitch done, blue twining threads are brought to the reverse of the fabric to be knotted. Blue and red beads are embroidered by simple couching stitch at random.

4 Release the embroidery-surface from the hoop. The embroidery fabric is placed in the center of cotton cloth with the same size and texture.

5 Turn the embroidery surface and the other piece of cloth inward and sew the rough fringes of the opening on three sides to create a bag. Completed.

8. Cup Mat of Tang Curling Flower Patterns

With an ingenious conception and distinctive feature, this embroidered cup mat presents a sense of magnificence. Its patterns are marked by progressive layers of rich decoration. The design proceeds from the inner part to the outer part in order, i.e. the stamen, eight petals, eight leaves, and a circle of cloud patterns. On the verge of the outermost flank, there are four patterns of Tang curling flowers and four single petals dotted in a crisscrossed manner.

You can either use the cup mat while drinking tea or just appreciate it like a piece of art.

The Size Suggested
13.5 ×13.5 cm

You Will Need
Embroidery needle: 9#
Embroidery fabric: sapphire blue satin damask
Embroidery threads:
    The stamen: blue silk threads
    The petal: orange silk threads and white silk threads
    The outer fringe of leaves and petals: gold threads and yellow sewing threads
    Tang curling flowers: gold threads and yellow sewing threads

Stitch Diagram
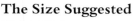 Straight satin stitch (page 46)
 Long and short shaded satin stitch (page 79)
 Gold thread couching stitch (page 58)

Stitch Guide

1 Apply blue silk threads and straight satin stitch to embroider the stamen. Use orange and white silk threads and long and short shaded satin stitch to embroider petals.

2 Use orange and white silk threads and long and short shaded satin stitch to embroider single petals on the verge around. Apply two strands of gold threads and yellow sewing threads and gold thread couching stitch to finish the verge on the outer flank of the cup mat. Be sure that the three layers on the verge is embroidered with two strands in each layer. The outermost golden layer happens to cover the outer-fringe of the single petals.

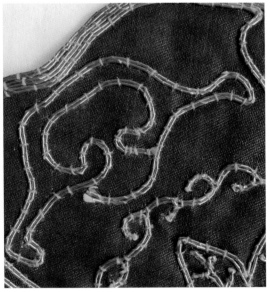

3 Apply gold threads and yellow sewing threads and gold thread couching stitch to finish the outer-fringe of the stamen, the outer-fringe of the petals, and leaves.

4 Apply gold threads and yellow sewing threads and gold thread couching stitch to finish the patterns of the Tang curling flowers and a circle of cloud patterns. With the embroidery completed, cut off a piece of lining cloth as large as the embroidery fabric to be sewn with the embroidery fabric to complete the cup mat.

9. Vase Mat with a Pattern Indicating Richness and Honors in Four Seasons

On this vase mat, there are three kinds of flowers representing different seasons, i.e. the peony in the middle denotes nobility, the plum blossom on the right stands for purity, and the magnolia on the left signifies outstanding talent. Coupled with patterns of floral scrolls embroidered by gold threads around, this vase mat indicates "prosperity in four seasons."

The Size Suggested
27.5 × 21.5 cm

You Will Need
Embroidery needle: 9#
Embroidery fabric: red satin damask
Back-cloth: as large as the embroidery fabric
Embroidery threads:

   Outer fringes and patterns of floral scrolls: gold threads and yellow sewing threads
   The inner fringes: silver threads and white sewing threads
   Petals (peony, plum blossom, and magnolia): silk threads of red shades
   Leaves (peony) and calyx (magnolia): silk threads of green shades
   Stems: silk threads of brown shades
   The stigma (the upper part of the plum blossom stamen) and the ovary (the lower part of the plum blossom stamen): silk threads of yellow shades
   The column (the middle part of the plum blossom stamen): dark green silk threads

Stitch Diagram
▩ Gold thread couching stitch (page 58)
▩ Silver thread couching stitch (page 58)
▩ ▩ Regular shaded satin stitch (page 78)
■ Slanted satin stitch (page 77)
■ Basic knot stitch (page 62)
■ Star stitch (page 80)

Stitch Guide

1 Apply gold thread couching stitch to complete fringes and patterns of floral scrolls at the outer flank. Use yellow sewing threads as tying threads to tack the gold threads.

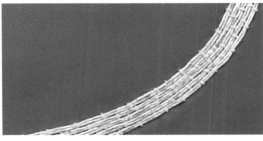

2 Apply silver thread couching stitch to complete the inner fringes. Use white sewing threads as tacking threads to tack the silver threads.

3 Apply regular shaded satin stitch with silk threads of red shades to complete the peony petals; use regular shaded satin stitch with silk threads of green shades to complete peony leaves.

4 Apply regular shaded satin stitch with silk threads of red shades to embroider the magnolia petals; use regular shaded satin stitch with silk threads of green shades to complete the magnolia calyx.

5 Apply regular shaded satin stitch with silk threads of red shades to complete the plum blossom petals; use the basic knot stitch with yellow silk threads to complete the stigma at the upper part of the stamen and the ovary at the lower part of the stamen. Use star stitch with dark green silk threads to embroider the column of the stamen.

6 Apply slanted satin stitch with brown silk threads to complete the stems of peony, plum blossom, and magnolia. After the embroidery is completed, cut a piece of back cloth as large as the vase mat. Sew it with the embroidery fabric and iron them flat. The vase mat is completed.

10. Flowers

Three kinds of needlework have been applied to this embroidered article with flower patterns, i.e. basic knot stitch, gold/silver thread couching stitch, and stem stitch. A variety of colors are alternately used in the patterns of the knot stitch that gives a lively effect. Gold/silver thread couching stitch is used to decorate two lines on the verge, further making the entire embroidery appear magnificent.

This embroidered article can be used to decorate such daily necessities as tablecloths, trunks, and bags, etc.

You Will Need
Embroidery needle: 9#
Embroidery fabric: light pea green plain woven silk fabric
Embroidery threads:

Golden outer-frame: gold threads and orange sewing threads
Silver frame-rim: silver threads and white sewing threads
Branches: gold threads and light blue sewing threads
Leaves: silk threads of green shades and blue shades
Flowers: red, blue, purple, white, orange, yellow, pink, brown, and green silk threads

Stitch Diagram

■ Stem stitch (page 51)

■ Simple couching stitch (refer to gold/silver thread couching stitch on page 58)

■ ■ ■ ■ ■ ■ ■ ■ Basic knot stitch (page 62)

■ ■ Gold/silver thread couching stitch (page 58)

Stitch Guide

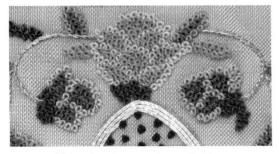

1 Use gold threads and stem stitch to embroider two symmetrical branches, and tack gold threads with light blue sewing threads by using simple couching stitch. Use silk threads of pink and purple shades and basic knot stitch to embroider flowers above symmetrical branches. Apply brown silk threads and basic knot stitch to embroider the calyx of flowers. Use silk threads of green and blue shades and basic knot stitch to embroider leaf blades on two symmetrical branches.

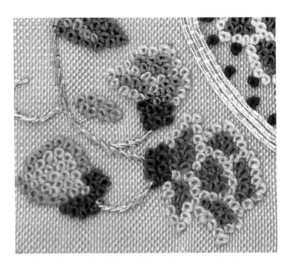

2 Use silk threads of blue, pink, and brown and basic knot stitch to embroider flowers at the tips of the two symmetrical branches. Apply silk threads of brown and basic knot stitch to embroider the calyx of flowers.

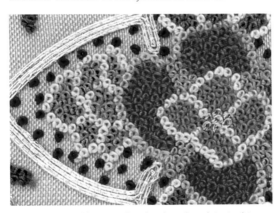

3 The four-leaf flower within the silver-thread rim in this embroidered article is divided into five layers from the inner part to the outer part, all embroidered by basic knot stitch. Gold threads, as well as yellow, green, orange, pink, blue, and burgundy silk threads are used respectively. Then, apply silver threads and white sewing threads and silver thread couching stitch to finish the frame-rim of the four-leaf flower with three layers.

4 Use gold threads, orange sewing threads, and gold thread couching stitch to finish the fringe-lines on the outer flank with three layers.

5 Completed.

11. Dandelion and Wild Chrysanthemum

Dandelions and wild chrysanthemums are perennial grass plants. Dandelions are marked by large leaves with fairly deep saw-tooth. The white florets on their seeds, blown by the wind to new places, give rise to new life. The leaves of wild chrysanthemums are triangular and the small petals are arranged in an array of umbrellas. Tube-like flowers are seen in the center of the petals with many branches of stems.

As a fresh style, dandelion and wild chrysanthemum patterns can be embroidered on a variety of daily necessities such as garments, handkerchiefs, tablecloths, and napkins.

You Will Need

Embroidery needle: 9#

Embroidery fabric: pale pinkish grey silk tabby

Embroidery threads:

Big dandelion leaves, dandelion petals, wild chrysanthemum petals: silk threads of orange shades

Small dandelion leaves and calyx, wild chrysanthemum leaves: silk threads of green shades

Dandelion stems and wild chrysanthemum stems: silk threads of white shades

Outlines and veins of big dandelion leaves and outlines of dandelion flowers: white silk threads

Wild chrysanthemum buds and dandelion stamens: silver silk threads

Wild chrysanthemum stamens: yellow silk threads

Stitch Diagram

■ Basic knot stitch (page 62)

■ Stem stitch (page 51)

■ Slanted satin stitch (page 77)

■ Straight satin stitch (page 46)

■ Split stitch (page 52)

Stitch Guide

2 Apply silk threads of orange shades and slanted satin stitch to embroider wild chrysanthemum petals. Use yellow silk threads and basic knot stitch to complete the wild chrysanthemum stamens. Apply white silk threads and slanted satin stitch to complete the stems. Apply silver silk threads and slanted satin stitch to complete the wild chrysanthemum buds.

1 Apply orange silk threads and basic knot stitch to complete the inside of the big dandelion leaves. Use white silk threads and stem stitch to embroider saw-tooth outlines and the veins of the big dandelion leaves.

3 Use silk threads of green shades and straight satin stitch to complete the wild chrysanthemum leaves. Apply white silk threads and slanted satin stitch to embroider the wild chrysanthemum stems.

4 Embroidery of dandelions: Apply silk threads of orange shades and straight satin stitch to complete the petals. Use silver silk threads and straight satin stitch to complete the stamens. Apply green silk threads and straight satin stitch to complete the calyx. Use white silk threads and split stitch as well as stem stitch to complete the flower outlines. Apply green silk threads and straight satin stitch to complete the small leaves. Use white silk threads and slanted satin stitch to embroider the stems.

12. Chinese Wisteria

The features of Chinese wisteria are zigzagging stems, vines, and dense purple flowers hung amidst green leaves and vines against the breeze. Chinese wisteria represents long life and wealth since it falls in the category of longevity as a tree species, hence enjoying great popularity among people.

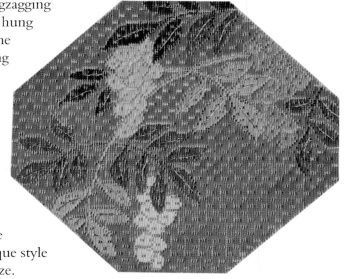

This embroidered article is an integration of counted stitch over gauze and stem stitch. Counted stitch over gauze is extensively applied in the embroidery of Chinese wisteria flowers, base patterns, and leaves. If the stitch fully covers the gauze, it is a unique style known as counted satin stitch over gauze.

You Will Need

Embroidery needle: 9#
Embroidery fabric: real silk gauze of 36 small square per inch
Embroidery threads:
    Base-color: silk threads of coffee color
    Stems and leaf blades: silk threads of green shades
    Leaf veins: gold threads
    Chinese wisteria flowers: silk threads of purple shades

Stitch Diagram

■ ■ ■ ■ ■ ■ Vertical counted stitch over gauze (page 65)
■ Stem stitch (page 51)

Stitch Guide

1 Use coffee color silk threads and vertical counted stitch over gauze to fully embroider the base color. In order to produce the effect of small squares, embroider three vertical stitches to leave three squares behind and then embroider another three vertical stitches to leave three squares behind. The process goes on like this repeatedly.

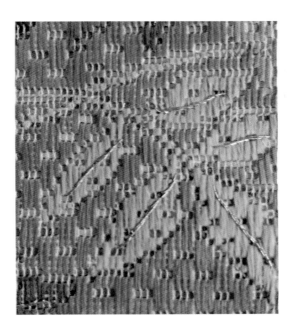

2 Apply silk threads of purple shades and vertical counted stitch over gauze to embroider three strings of Chinese wisteria. Be sure that stitches are in different length and some empty squares are exposed between each flower petals in order to differentiate them.

3 Use silk threads of green shades and vertical counted stitch over gauze to embroider leaf blades. As for bigger leaf blades, there should be two stitches in a vertical direction with one square set between two stitches. Then apply gold threads and stem stitch to embroider leaf veins on leaf blades. Use light green silk threads and vertical counted stitch over gauze to embroider stems.

13. Fortune Peony

In China, peony is always recognized as "the king of flowers." Its dignified and plump form, gorgeous color, and strong fragrance signifies wealth. Patterns of this embroidered article are very suitable for the front part of a lady's evening gown with spaghetti straps.

You Will Need
Embroidery needle: 9#
Embroidery fabric: purple satin damask
Embroidery threads:
    Petals and the stamen: silk threads of pink shades
    Leaves and leaf veins: silk threads of green shades
    Stems: light brown silk threads
    Outer fringes of petals: gold threads and light pink sewing threads

Stitch Diagram
■ ■ Regular shaded satin stitch (page 78)   ▨ ▨ Slanted satin stitch (page 77)
■ Basic knot stitch (page 62)   ▨ Split stitch (page 52)
■ Gold thread couching stitch (page 58)

Stitch Guide

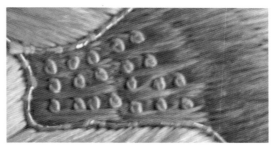

1 Use silk threads of pink shades and regular shaded satin stitch to embroider peony petals. The four narrower petals should be embroidered by light pink silk threads and slanted satin stitch, i.e. four narrow petals on the verge of petals on the outer flank of the big peony in the center.

2 Use the lightest of pink silk threads and basic knot stitch to embroider the stamen of the big peony in the center.

3 Apply gold threads, light pink sewing threads, and gold thread couching stitch to embroider the outer-fringe of the big peony.

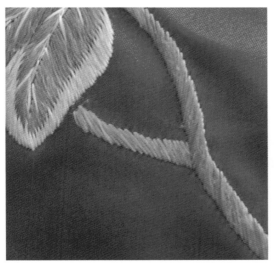

4 Use light brown silk threads and slanted satin stitch to embroider the stems.

5 Apply silk threads of green shades and regular shaded satin stitch to embroider leaves. Use the lightest of green silk threads and split stitch to embroider leaf veins.

14. The Miao Ethnicity Embroidery with Patterns of Butterfly and Flower

As its name implies, the Ethnic Embroidery of the Miao (*miao xiu*) is a craftsmanship handed down by people of the Miao ethnicity in China. Its features are bright colors, dense patterns, vivid design, symmetrical and harmonious picture composition, and natural forms.

This embroidered article is an integration of deformed butterflies and flowers. Butterfly is Miao people's most favorite pattern. In Miao's legends, the butterfly created human beings and symbolizes the extension of the Miao ethnicity. As a very decorative article, it can be used to embroider the sleeve-fringe of a young woman's apparel or baby carriers.

You Will Need
Embroidery needle: 9#
Embroidery fabric: black cotton cloth
Embroidery threads:
  Butterfly antenna and the outline of butterflies and deformed flowers: white twining threads and white sewing threads
  Butterflies: silk threads of red shades, green, and yellow silk threads
  Flowers: silk threads of red shades, green, yellow, and blue silk threads

Stitch Diagram
■ Twining thread couching stitch (page 81)
■ ■ ■ Straight bullion knot (page 84)

Stitch Guide

1 Use white twining threads, white sewing threads, and twining thread couching stitch to embroider the outline of butterflies and flowers.

2 Apply silk threads of red shades, yellow, and green silk threads and straight bullion knot to embroider butterfly wings and the butterfly body in the middle of the pattern.

3 Use silk threads of red and blue shades and straight bullion knot to embroider deformed flowers on both sides of the big butterfly.

4 Apply silk threads of red and blue shades, green and yellow silk threads and straight bullion knot to embroider round deformed flowers at both ends of the pattern and small butterflies in the flower. Silk threads of red shades, yellow, and green silk threads as well as straight bullion knot are used to embroider the buds at the outermost of the pattern.

15. Lady's Handbag with Patterns of Butterfly and Flower

Works which we introduced previously are all marked by patterns drawn on paper first and then transferred to the embroidery fabric according to the method introduced in Chapter Two. However, this embroidered article is slightly different, i.e. the pattern drawn on paper is cut off to be attached to the embroidery fabric before embroidery starts.

With the paper-pattern as the foil, patterns embroidered will be exceptionally full and attractive and fit the surface very well. The combination of abstract butterflies and flowers on a small female handbag is very fashionable.

The Size Suggested

23 × 23 cm

You Will Need

Embroidery needle: 9#
Embroidery fabric: green cotton cloth
Embroidery threads:
  The outline of butterflies and flowers: gold threads and white sewing threads
  The body and antenna of butterflies: light purple and yellow silk threads
  Butterfly wings: red, blue silk threads and silk threads of purple shades
  Deformed flowers: silk threads of purple, green and red shades, and blue silk threads

Stitch Diagram

 Gold thread couching stitch (page 58)
Long and short shaded satin stitch (page 79)
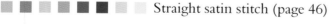 Straight satin stitch (page 46)

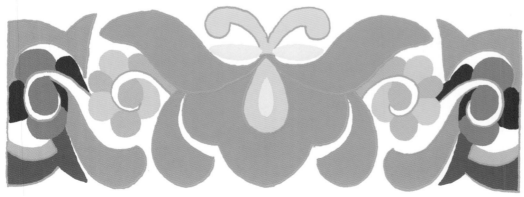

Stitch Guide

1 Cut off the sketch to be attached to the green embroidery fabric until it is completely dry.

2 Use gold threads, white sewing threads, and gold thread couching stitch to embroider the outline of butterflies and deformed flowers. Or you can embroider the inner patterns first and use gold thread couching stitch to finish the outlines at last.

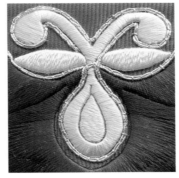

4 Use light purple and yellow silk threads as well as straight satin stitch to embroider the body and antenna of butterflies.

3 Red and blue silk threads and silk threads of purple shades and long and short shaded satin stitch are applied to embroider butterfly wings.

5 Apply green and light red silk threads and straight satin stitch to embroider scrolling-leaf-like abstract flowers beside the butterfly. Silk threads of purple, red, green shades and blue silk threads and straight satin stitch are used to embroider abstract flowers on both sides of the pattern.

6 The completed embroidery is sewn on the handbag.

16. Embroidered Pouch of the Shui Ethnicity

As one of the ethnic minorities in China, the Shuis are mainly in the south and southeast of Guizhou Province. Pouches are small bags carried by people to hold small articles which are daily necessities of the Shui people. With a rich variety of styles, there are simple ones like round, oval, square, and oblong pouches as well as complicated ones like peach-shaped, *ruyi*-shaped, and pomegranate-shaped pouches, etc. Now, we will introduce how to make a pomegranate-shaped pouch.

The horse-tail-hair twining thread couching stitch of the Shui is quite unique. Horse-tail-hair is twined with white threads with which pre-designed patterns are embroidered, thus forming outlines. Within these outlines, different patterns are embroidered with various kinds of colorful silk threads. Embroidered articles have a sense of cameo and uniqueness with their distinctive ethnic features.

Prior to embroidery, the bright red cotton cloth is reversed and starched by a thin paste to increase the stiffness of the pouch. The embroidery fabric can be held in hand without the need of a hoop.

The Size Suggested
The cover: 10.7 × 6.7 cm
The body: 10.7 × 12.5 cm

Stitch Diagram
■ Twining thread couching stitch (page 81)
■ ■ Weaving stitch (page 68)
■ ■ Blanket stitch (page 47)
■ ■ ■ Coiling stitch (page 82)

You Will Need

Embroidery needle: 9#

Embroidery fabric: bright red cotton cloth (the pouch-surface) and dark blue cotton cloth (the inner layer of the pouch)

Embroidery threads:

The outer-fringe of patterns: white twining threads and white tacking threads

Patterns: brown, purple, rosy, and green silk threads

Trapezium border on the upper part of the cover and arc-shaped border on the lower part of the body: green and orange silk threads

Wave-shaped border on the lower part of the cover: blue silk threads

Stitch Guide

The Cover

1 White twining threads, white sewing threads, and twining thread couching stitch are used to complete the outline of flower patterns. Brown, purple, rosy, and green silk threads and coiling stitch are applied to fill in the inner part of the flower patterns.

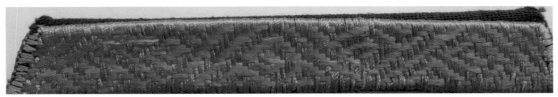

2 Green and orange silk threads and weaving stitch are used to embroider the rectangular spiral patterns on trapezium border on the upper part of the cover.

3 Apply green silk threads and blanket stitch to embroider another two borders as reinforcement along the fringe at both ends of the trapezium border.

4 Use blue silk threads and blanket stitch to embroider the wave-shaped border on the lower part of the cover to cover the rough fringe of embroidery fabric.

5 The cover has been completed through embroidery.

The Body

6 White twining threads, white sewing threads, and twining thread couching stitch are applied to tack the outline of flower patterns. Brown, purple, rosy, and green silk threads and coiling stitch are used to fill in the inner part of flower patterns.

7 Green and orange silk threads and weaving stitch are applied to embroider the rectangular spiral patterns on the arc-shaped border on the lower part of the body.

8 Green silk threads and blanket stitch are applied to embroider another two borders as reinforcement along the fringe at both ends of the arc-shaped border.

To Be Sewn

9 The pouch-body has been completed through embroidery.

10 Dark blue cotton cloth is cut into the pouch-lining according to the size of the embroidery fabric. Then embroidered cover and embroidered body are sewn to complete the piece.

17. Pillow Cover with a Pattern of Blessing of Many Children and Good Fortune

In ancient China, the cover at both ends of the pillow was square and mostly embroidered with exquisite flowers.

This pattern is called "Blessing of Many Children and Good Fotune" chiefly composed of pomegranates. Thanks to lots of seeds inside, the pomegranate represents many children. In ancient times, this indicated a kind of good fortune. In the middle of the pattern, two big pomegranates at the upper and the lower parts constitute the shape of a calabash. Because of the many vines, the calabash denotes longevity. Also the first Chinese character of calabash is a homonym of good fortune. On the yellow vines, there are small pomegranates and pomegranate flowers of many colors.

The Size Suggested
17 × 17.5 cm

You will need

Embroidery needle: 9#

Embroidery fabric: black satin damask

Embroidery threads:

Pomegranate buds: cotton threads of peach-red shades

Small pomegranates: apricot-yellow cotton threads and green cotton threads

Big pomegranates: peach-red cotton threads

Stems: cream-colored cotton threads and peach-red cotton threads

Leaves: cotton threads of green shades and purple cotton threads

Pomegranate seeds: cotton threads of green shades

The inside of the pomegranate: apricot-yellow cotton threads and cotton threads of red shades

Pomegranate stamen: cotton threads of green shades

Stitch Diagram

■ Slanted satin stitch (page 77)

■ Straight satin stitch (page 46)

■ Shaded satin stitch (page 78)

■ Flower pattern blanket stitch (page 49)

■ Star stitch (page 80)

Stitch Guide

1 Apply cotton threads of green shades and slanted satin stitch to complete the leaves; use cream-colored cotton threads and slanted satin stitch to complete the stems.

2 Apply apricot-yellow cotton threads and straight satin stitch to complete small pomegranates; use peach-red cotton threads and slanted satin stitch to embroider the root of stems.

3 Use cotton threads of peach-red shades and shaded satin stitch to complete the pomegranate buds; use cotton threads of green shades and flower pattern blanket stitch to complete the pomegranate seeds; apply cotton threads of green shades and star stitch to bring about pomegranate stamen.

4 Apply cotton threads of green shades and slanted satin stitch to complete the small leaves between small pomegranates and buds.

6 Use cotton threads of peach-red shades and slanted satin stitch to embroider the pomegranate shells. Use apricot-yellow cotton threads and slanted satin stitch to complete the arc inside at two places. Apply cotton threads of red shades and shaded satin stitch to complete the spindle-shaped pomegranate core. Use cotton threads of green shades and flower pattern blanket stitch to complete the pomegranate seeds. Use cotton threads of green shades and star stitch to complete the straight lines at the upper part of the spindle-shaped core.

5 Apply cotton threads of peach-red shades and slanted satin stitch to complete the pomegranate shells. Use cotton threads of red shades and straight satin stitch to embroider the upper part of the inside of the pomegranate. Use cotton threads of red shades and shaded satin stitch to complete the lower part of the inside of the pomegranate. Apply cotton threads of green shades and flower pattern blanket stitch to embroider pomegranate seeds. Use cotton threads of green shades and start stitch to complete the petal-tips and stamens.

7 Apply cotton threads of green shades and straight satin stitch to complete the small pomegranates. A piece of sequin can be attached to the pomegranate. Completed.

18. Two Dragons Playing the Ball

It is a pattern of two dragons playing with (or trying to seize) a fireball. In this pattern, one dragon is on the left and the other is on the right, with the fireball in between. In the Ming Dynasty and the Qing Dynasty, such a pattern was quite popular as it was often seen on the jewels, garments, and shoes of nobles, signifying auspiciousness and festive celebration.

There are patterns of rolling seawater below this embroidered article. Such patterns could often be seen on the lower hem of the dragon robe and official gown in ancient China. Curved lines stand for rolling waves. There is a rock in the water decorated by auspicious clouds, connoting the mountain of happiness and the sea of longevity as well as unification of China.

You Will Need
Embroidery needle: 9#
Embroidery fabric: red real silk satin damask
Embroidery threads:
  The dragon: silk threads of blue and green shades, light red, black, apricot, and white silk threads
  The fireball: light red silk threads
  Rolling seawater: silk threads of red, green, yellow and blue shades

Stitch Diagram
■ Straight satin stitch (page 46)
■ Net stitch (page 61)
■ ■ ■ ■ ■ ■ ■ ■ Slanted satin stitch (page 77)
■ ■ Basic encroaching satin stitch (page 55)
■ Split stitch (page 52)

Stitch Guide

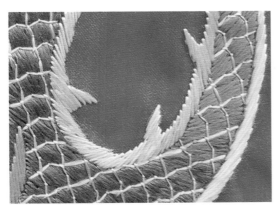

1 Blue silk threads and straight satin stitch are used to embroider the dragon's body. White silk threads and net stitch are applied to embroider the scales. White silk threads and slanted satin stitch are applied to embroider the outline of the body.

3 Blue and white silk threads as well as slanted satin stitch are used to embroider the dragon's claws.

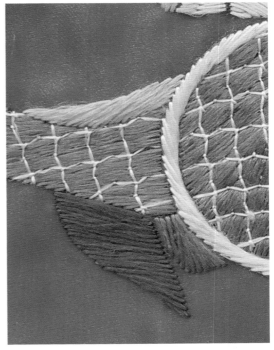

2 Blue silk threads and straight satin stitch are used to embroider the dragon's legs. White silk threads and net stitch are applied to embroider scales on the legs. Slanted satin stitch is used to embroider green and apricot color hair on the dragon.

4 Blue and white silk threads and basic encroaching satin stitch are applied to embroider the dragon's head. White and black silk threads and basic encroaching satin stitch are used to embroider the eyes. Silk threads of apricot color and slanted satin stitch are applied to embroider the mouth and the tongue. White silk threads and slanted satin stitch are used to embroider the teeth. White silk threads and slanted satin stitch are applied to embroider the horns. Silk threads of green shades and apricot color silk threads and slanted satin stitch are used to embroider the hair.

5 White silk threads and slanted satin stitch are used to embroider the thick dragon's beard near the mouth. Split stitch is applied to embroider fine and curved beard.

6 White silk threads and slanted satin stitch are used to embroider the dragon's tail.

7 The fireball is completely embroidered by silk threads of apricot color. Slanted satin stitch is applied to embroider the outer frame of the fireball and radiating flame. Straight satin stitch is used to embroider five round dots inside the fireball.

8 Silk threads of red, blue, green and yellow shades and white silk threads and slanted satin stitch are used to embroider curved waves and square rocks. White silk threads and straight satin stitch are applied to embroider water drops above the sea.

19. Silk Scarf with Multi-Flower Pattern

Patterns on the left and the right of this silk scarf are symmetrical, with Part 4 as the center, i.e. there are flowers in three groups with the same patterns on each side, altogether seven groups. Though only three kinds of needlework are applied, it looks magnificent thanks to a rich variety of colors and full patterns. Now, we will introduce one of the most complex integrations as follows. You can do it accordingly with the same method.

The Size Suggested
52 × 170 cm

You Will Need
Embroidery needle: 9#
Embroidery fabric: red real silk crepe de chine
Embroidery threads:
    Leaf blades: silk threads of green and brown shades
    Flowers: silk threads of red, blue, yellow, pink, and purple shades
    Stems: silk threads of brown shades

Stitch Diagram
- ◼ Slanted stain stitch (page 77)
- ◼ Straight satin stitch (page 46)
- ◼ Regular shaded satin stitch (page 78)

Part 1

Part 2

Part 3

Part 4

Stitch Guide (with Part 2 as an Example)

1 Silk threads of green shades and slanted satin stitch are used to embroider green leaves. Silk threads of red shades and slanted satin stitch are used to embroider small flowers in blossom on the left upper corner. Blue and purple silk threads, as well as straight satin stitch, are applied to embroider daisies. Red, purple, and yellow silk threads are used respectively to embroider three small round buds on the lower part. Yellow silk threads and straight satin stitch are applied to embroider the stamen of Chinese pink on the right upper part. Then regular shaded satin stitch is used to embroider the petals of Chinese pink.

2 Use silk threads of green shades and slanted satin stitch to embroider leaves. Use silk threads of brown shades and slanted satin stitch to embroider stems. Use silk threads of yellow shades and straight satin stitch to embroider the yellow daisies and two small yellow buds. Use silk threads of purple shades and straight satin stitch to embroider the purple daisy. Use silk threads of red shades and straight satin stitch to embroider two small round buds on the left lower part of the small purple daisy.

3 Use silk threads of red shades and regular shaded satin stitch to embroider the outermost petals of the big peony at the center. Use straight satin stitch to embroider the petals in the center of this big peony.

4 Use silk threads of brown shades and slanted satin stitch to embroider stems. Use silk threads of green shades and slanted satin stitch to embroider leaves. Use yellow, blue, and red silk threads as well as straight satin stitch to embroider six small round buds. Use silk threads of red shades and straight satin stitch to embroider the stamen of Chinese pink first. Then apply regular shaded satin stitch to embroider petals.

5 Use purple silk threads and straight satin stitch to embroider the small bud on the lower part of the peony. Use silk threads of pink shades and regular shaded satin stitch to embroider the outermost petals of the peony. Use silk threads of red shades and straight satin stitch to embroider petals of the second layers. Then apply slanted satin stitch to embroider the inner petals.

6 Use purple silk threads and straight satin stitch to embroider two small round buds. Use silk threads of red shades and straight satin stitch to embroider the red daisy. Use blue silk threads and straight satin stitch to embroider the blue Chinese pink. Use silk threads of green shades and slanted satin stitch to embroider leaves. Use silk threads of brown shades and slanted satin stitch to embroider stems.

7 Use silk threads of yellow shades and straight satin stitch to embroider the small round bud on the upper part of the yellow chrysanthemum. Use silk threads of yellow shades and regular shaded satin stitch to embroider the chrysanthemum. Use silk threads of green shades and slanted satin stitch to embroider leaves. Use silk threads of brown shades and slanted satin stitch to embroider stems.

8 Use silk threads of green shades and slanted satin stitch to embroider leaves. Use brown silk threads and slanted satin stitch to embroider stems. Use blue silk threads and slanted satin stitch to embroider the outermost small oval bud. Use brown silk threads and straight satin stitch to embroider the calyx of the small blue bud. Use silk threads of red shades and straight satin stitch to embroider two small round buds on both sides of the blue bud. Use silk threads of red shades and straight satin stitch to embroider the red Chinese pink.

9 Use silk threads of green shades and slanted satin stitch to embroider leaves. Use silk threads of brown shades and slanted satin stitch to embroider stems. Use silk threads of yellow shades and straight satin stitch to embroider two small yellow round buds. Use silk threads of purple shades and slanted satin stitch to embroider the small purple round bud. Use silk threads of red shades and slanted satin stitch to embroider a small red flower on the upper part and a small oval bud below it.

10 The embroidery of Part 2 is complete.

11 It runs from parts 1, 2, 3 from the bottom to the top. Then, the above mentioned method is applied to embroider the patterns of parts 1, 2, and 3 on the other half as well as the pattern of Part 4 in the center.

12 With embroidery done, both ends of the silk scarf are decorated with tassels of the same color to reinforce the sense of suspension. Completed.

CHAPTER FIVE
ARTISTIC EMBROIDERY PROJECTS

Along with constant innovation of needlework for embroidery, continuous development of embroidery of daily life and ongoing enhancement of people's aesthetic standards, embroidered articles have gradually developed from crafts to artistic works. Embroidered articles are as exquisite as paintings for public appreciation.

High standards are set on embroidery for appreciation, resulting in complex craftsmanship. Usually, only those who have gone through strict training can reach standards of qualification.

Three projects will be introduced in this chapter. For beginners, it is enough to acquire some understanding through reading and give it a try with confidence. Exquisiteness of embroidered articles produced by them is not a must. For those with considerable basic technique of embroidery, they should earnestly experience wonderful craftsmanship of different kinds of needlework and free themselves from the needlework. Readers may try to embroider an article for appreciation according to their actual technical level.

FIG. 49 *Mountain-Magpies and Loquats* by Shao Xiaocheng (Complete)
Song Dynasty Embroidery
Private Collection, USA
It was produced according to a famous painting of the same name in the Song Dynasty. This embroidered article is featured by needlework of Song Dynasty embroidery, showing the meticulous and detailed style of the paintings in the Song Dynasty. Two blue mountain-magpies leaning close to each other are marked by a variety of needlework, having plump, soft, fine, and dense feathers as well as bright and gorgeous hair. Loquats are round and sleek, ready to be mature with much freshness in the color. Traces on tree-leaves bitten by insects are vivid. The entire embroidered article is quite spirited with grace and elegance, immediately leaving an impression of antiquity.

1. Amused Children

Natural hair is used as threads for such embroidery. Hair is featured by an elegant tint, also free from insect-bites, decay and color fading, hence being able to make the embroidered article as exquisite and elegant as a meticulous painting and express the charm of ink color. This embroidered article shows a number of children gaming and playing hide and seek. Each of them is marked by a rich facial expression, cleverness, and quick mindedness. Though there are not many colors, the liveliness of these children is revealed by superb embroidery skills. While enjoying them, viewers may gain a child-like heart and feel active along with the movements of the children.

Your hair and the hair of your relatives and friends can be used as hair threads, or you can buy it from the hairdresser's. It's better to use the hair from those who have just had their hair washed and cut off, because hair will be in disorder if it is cut off first before it is washed. It is OK if the hair is 30 centimeters long. Hair treated with cream, permed or dyed or softened should not be used. First, it is not environmentally friendly. Second, it is not good for preserving the hair embroidery works.

The Size Suggested
50 × 90 cm

You Will Need
Embroidery needle: 9#
Embroidery fabric: cream-colored plain woven real silk
Embroidery threads:
    The mouths, noses, ears, and eyes of the children: fairly fine hair
    Scenes and objects held by the child: fairly thick black hair
    The golden fish: hair of light color

Needlework
Stem stitch (page 51)
Split stitch (page 52)
Straight satin stitch
(page 46)
Shaded satin stitch
(page 78)
Simple couching stitch
(refer to gold/silver
thread couching stitch
on page 58)

Stitch Technique
Each line of hair embroidery should be able to represent its connotation. It is not allowed to make the line a lifeless and dull one. The beginning and the end of each line should be able to express the artistic language of Chinese ink sketch. It is not allowed to turn the line into the same thickness or make it appear mechanical like the woodcutting. The eyebrows and eyes of the child should look vivid and expressive through different shades.

Stitch Guide

1 Use the fine hair, stem stitch, and split stitch to embroider the child and the wrinkled lines of his clothes. Apply simple couching stitch and split stitch to embroider his hair bun. Use straight satin stitch to embroider the handle in his hand. Then apply shaded satin stitch to embroider the downy part over the object held in his left hand and the cirrus-shaped tail of the object held in his right hand. Use shaded satin stitch to embroider his shoes.

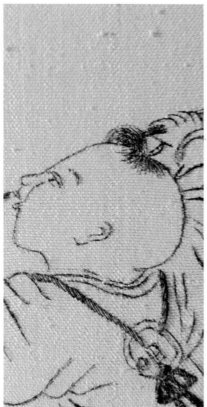

2 (Left and above) Use the fine hair, stem stitch, and split stitch to embroider the child and wrinkled lines of his clothes. Use simple couching stitch and split stitch to embroider his hair bun. Use shaded satin stitch to embroider his shoes. Use shaded satin stitch to embroider the *ruyi* pendent on his back. Use straight satin stitch to embroider the handle of the feather duster held in his hands. Then use shaded satin stitch to embroider the downy part over this duster.

3 (Right and far right) Use the fine hair, stem stitch, and split stitch to embroider the child and wrinkled lines of his clothes. Apply simple couching stitch and split stitch to embroider his hair bun. Use shaded satin stitch to embroider his shoes. Use shaded satin stitch to embroider tassels of the pendent on his chest. Use stem stitch and split stitch to embroider the outline of the flag in his hand and the wrinkled lines on the flag. Apply straight satin stitch and shaded satin stitch to embroider the flagpole, triangle fringes, and the decorative belt.

4 Use stem stitch and split stitch to embroider the child and wrinkled lines of his clothes. Use simple couching stitch and split stitch to embroider his hair bun. Use straight satin stitch to embroider the mask. Use stem stitch and split stitch to embroider the outline of the writing brush held in his right hand and then apply straight satin stitch to embroider the hair of the writing brush. Apply straight satin stitch to embroider his shoes. Use stem stitch and split stitch to embroider the outline of the heated ink slab held in his left hand. Then use shaded satin stitch to embroider the surface of the heated ink slab. Use stem stitch and split stitch to embroider the outline of the small table trampled by his right foot and the outline of the small stool on the left of the small table. Use straight satin stitch and shaded satin stitch to embroider the table corner and table fringe. Apply shaded satin stitch to embroider the patterns on the marble table surface.

5 Use stem stitch and split stitch to embroider the child and the wrinkled lines of his clothes. Apply simple couching stitch and split stitch to embroider his hair bun. Use stem stitch and split stitch to embroider the outline of the objects held in his right hand and left hand. Then use straight satin stitch and shaded satin stitch to fully embroider the inner part of the object.

6 (Left) Use stem stitch and split stitch to embroider the child and the wrinkled lines of his clothes. Apply simple couching stitch and split stitch to embroider his hair bun. Apply straight satin stitch to embroider his shoes. Use straight satin stitch to embroider two bracelets over his wrists. Use stem stitch and split stitch to embroider the drum in front of him. Use straight satin stitch to embroider three stands at the lower part of the drum.

7 (Right) Use stem stitch and split stitch to embroider the child and the wrinkled lines of his clothes. Apply simple couching stitch and split stitch to embroider his hair bun. Use straight satin stitch to embroider the decorative belt of the pendent on his back. Apply straight satin stitch and shaded satin stitch to embroider the long feather duster held in his left hand.

8 (Left) Use stem stitch and split stitch to embroider the child and the wrinkled lines of his clothes. Apply simple couching stitch and split stitch to embroider his hair bun. Apply straight satin stitch to embroider the shoes of the younger child. Use shaded satin stitch to embroider the decorative belt of the pendent on the chest of the bigger child. Apply straight satin stitch, stem stitch, split stitch and simple couching stitch to embroider the dragonfly and the string in the right hand of the smaller child.

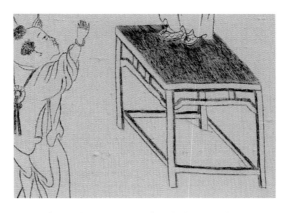

9 Apply straight satin stitch and shaded satin stitch to embroider the table trampled by two children.

10 (Left) Use stem stitch and split stitch to embroider the children and the wrinkled lines of the clothes of the three children. Apply simple couching stitch and split stitch to embroider their hair buns. Use stem stitch and split stitch to embroider the outline of the fish jar. Use light color fine hair, split stitch, and stem stitch to embroider the golden fish and water weeds in the jar. Use horizontal sparse stitch to embroider water ripples. Apply fairly thick black hair and shaded satin stitch to embroider the wood stand of the fish jar. Use straight satin stitch to embroider the necklet on the chest of the child in the middle and his shoes. Use straight satin stitch and shaded satin stitch to embroider the rough fringe on the clothes of the first child.

11 Use stem stitch and split stitch to embroider the child and the wrinkled lines of his clothes. Apply simple couching stitch and split stitch to embroider his hair bun. Apply straight satin stitch to embroider his shoes. Use straight satin stitch to embroider the front of his coat in crisscrossed patterns. Use shaded satin stitch to embroider the piece of cloth over his eyes.

12 Use stem stitch and split stitch to embroider the child and the wrinkled lines of his clothes. Apply simple couching stitch and split stitch to embroider his hair bun. Use shaded satin stitch to embroider the decorative belt of the pendent on his chest. Use straight satin stitch to embroider his shoes. Use stem stitch and split stitch to embroider the outline of the lantern. Use straight satin stitch and shaded satin stitch to embroider the handle and the pattern on the lantern. Use stem stitch and split stitch to embroider the outline of the miniature pot with rockery. Use straight satin stitch and shaded satin stitch to embroider the concave and convex parts as well as shaded parts of the rockery. Use straight satin stitch to embroider sedges below the rockery in the pot.

2. A Colorful Flower Basket

The completion of this embroidered article is chiefly attributed to the application of gold/silver thread couching stitch. Bright gold and silver threads coupled with tacking threads of various colors have not only brought brilliance to the lotus flower, chrysanthemum, day lily, and Chinese pink, but also reflected unique tints. Be sure that when embroidering each flower, please couch gold threads from the inside to the outside while tacking it.

The Size Suggested
30 cm in diameter

You Will Need
Embroidery needle: 9#
Embroidery fabric: black satin damask.
Embroidery threads:
  The flower basket: gold threads, yellow, red, and green sewing threads
  Daisies in the flower basket: gold and silver threads, as well as peach-red, green, orange, purple, and red sewing threads
  The chrysanthemum: gold threads and red sewing threads
  The peony: gold and silver threads, as well as red and purple sewing threads

The lotus flower: gold and silver threads, as well as purple, peach-red, and red sewing threads

The lotus leaf: gold threads and green sewing threads

The day lily: silver threads and peach-red sewing threads

The stamen of day lily: gold threads and red sewing threads

Petal veins of day lily: orange sewing threads

Buds of day lily: gold threads as well as purple and red sewing threads

Chinese pink: gold and silver threads as well as orange and purple sewing threads

Three-pronged leaf blades: gold and silver threads as well as green and blue sewing threads

Three-pronged leaf blades and veins: gold and silver threads as well as yellow sewing threads

Oblong leaf blades: gold and silver threads as well as green and blue sewing threads

Needlework

Gold/silver thread couching stitch (page 58)

Straight satin stitch (page 46)

Stitch Technique

The embroidery of each flower is completed by couching from the inside to the outside along with tacking. Two strands of gold threads or silver threads are used to do it, with these two strands tacked at the same time. When it comes to the turn, two strands of gold thread or silver thread should be separated for couching and tacking to make the turn natural and attractive. Then two strands of gold threads or silver threads are applied with these two strands tacked at the same time.

Stitch Guide

2 The handle, bow knot, and two ribbons of the flower basket are embroidered by gold thread couching stitch. Yellow sewing threads are used to tack the handle. Peach-red sewing threads are applied to tack the bow knot. Green sewing threads are used to tack ribbons on both sides.

1 The flower basket is completely embroidered by gold thread couching stitch, but colors of tacking threads are slightly different. Yellow sewing threads are used to tack the squares of the basket. Red sewing threads are applied to tack the inner border of the basket cover. Peach-red sewing threads are used to tack the decorative border of the basket cover. Red sewing threads are used to the tack the 8-shaped decorative borders in the middle of the basket as well as the circle at the bottom of it.

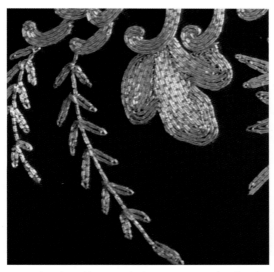

4 Leaves are embroidered by gold/silver thread couching stitch and tacked respectively by green and blue sewing threads. Leaf veins are embroidered by gold thread couching stitch and tacked by yellow sewing threads.

3 Wicker-shaped leaves at the lower part are embroidered by silver thread couching stitch and tacked by green sewing threads. Three leaves on the right of the leaves are embroidered by silver thread couching stitch and tacked by green sewing threads. Leaf veins are embroidered by gold thread couching stitch and tacked by red sewing threads.

5 Oblong leaf blades are embroidered by gold thread couching stitch and tacked by green and blue sewing threads.

6 Day lily petals are embroidered by silver thread couching
   stitch and tacked by purple sewing threads. The stamen
is embroidered by gold thread couching stitch and tacked by
orange sewing threads. Three long and oval buds below the
day lily are embroidered by gold thread couching stitch and
two of them on the left are tacked by purple sewing threads,
while another bud on the right is tacked by peach-red sewing
threads. The stem is embroidered by gold thread couching
stitch and tacked by green sewing threads. Apply orange
sewing threads and straight satin stitch to embroider a straight-
line pattern at the center of each day lily petal.

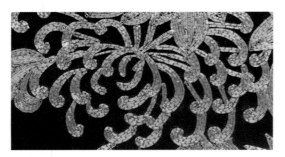

7 The chrysanthemum is embroidered by gold thread
   couching stitch and tacked by red sewing threads.

8 Daisies are embroidered by gold/silver thread couching
   stitch, tacked by green, purple, peach-red, orange, and blue
sewing threads.

9 Peony petals are embroidered by gold thread couching stitch and tacked by red sewing threads. Seven narrow petals amidst the peony petals are embroidered by silver thread couching stitch and tacked by purple sewing threads. Leaves are embroidered by gold/silver thread couching stitch and tacked by blue and green sewing threads. Leaf veins are embroidered by gold thread couching stitch and tacked by yellow sewing threads. The stem is embroidered by gold thread couching stitch and tacked by yellow sewing threads.

10 The big Chinese pink is embroidered by silver thread couching stitch and tacked by orange sewing threads. The small Chinese pink is embroidered by gold thread couching stitch and tacked by purple sewing threads.

11 The lotus flower is embroidered by silver thread couching stitch and tacked by purple and peach-red sewing threads. The lotus leaf is embroidered by gold thread couching stitch and tacked by green sewing threads. The upper orchid flower is embroidered by gold thread couching stitch and tacked by peach-red sewing threads. The lower orchid flower is embroidered by silver thread couching stitch and tacked by purple sewing threads. Oblong orchid leaf blades are respectively embroidered by gold/silver thread couching stitch, with gold threads tacked by green sewing threads and silver threads tacked by blue sewing threads.

3. Scenery of the Dai Ethnicity Village

As one of the ethnic minorities in China, the Dai people are seen in the sub-tropic area in the southwest of China. All villages of the Dai ethnic minority are in the vicinity of rivers with verdant trees around. The annual mean temperature in these areas is 21℃, marked by moisture and heat, only with difference of rainy and dry seasons. Located near the mountains and covered with various vegetation, these areas are rich in bamboo, leading to many pile dwelling built with bamboos and woods. Each dwelling is a single unit with space around. Each household has its own courtyard covered by tall trees. Women of the Dai ethnic minority usually appear slim. They are fond of having their hair bound as well as wearing narrow-sleeve short coats and cylinder-shaped skirts, fully revealing their slender figures.

In this scenic painting, the bamboo pile dwelling is encircled by plantains, palm trees, and coconut trees as well as a murmuring stream. Two girls are washing hair by the stream. The whole picture looks watery and foggy to the full, showing the local customs of the village of the Dai ethnic minority in the sub-tropic area.

Since this is embroidery for appreciation, the embroidered article can be mounted on or into the picture frame.

The Size Suggested
40 (H) × 50 (W) cm

You Will Need
Embroidery needle: 9#
Embroidery fabric: white satin damask
Embroidery threads:
  The sky: silk threads of white grades and pearlescent aqua shades
  The flood land: silk threads of white shades, brown shades, pearlescent aqua shades, and yellow shades
  A small waterfall: silk threads of white shades, green shades, and brown shades
  Hardy banana: silk threads of white shades, brown shades, green shades and pearlescent aqua shades
  Palm trees and coconut trees: silk threads of pearlescent aqua shades and brown shades
  Other trees: silk threads of green shades, yellow shades, and brown shades
  Bamboo pile dwelling: silk threads of brown shades, pearlescent aqua shades, and white shades
  Girls of the Dai ethnic minority and a water jar: black silk threads, red silk threads, silk threads of yellow shades, white shades, and brown shades
  The staircase: silk threads of white shades and brown shades

Needlework
Big free cross stitch (page 87)
Small free cross stitch (page 87)
Hash tag mark free cross stitch (page 87)

Stitch Technique
Since the color of this embroidery surface is required to be rich and dignified, but not showy, the color should not be applied haphazardly and densely in the course of embroidery. In the process of embroidery, attention should be paid to take into account the reasonable space, the richness, and rationality of the color.

Different colors should be added while this piece of work is being embroidered. Overlapped threads endow embroidery with the thickness of an oil painting and a sense of gradation. Threads split into six strands embroider the first layer. Five or three strands will be used when the color is multiplied in the course of embroidery. Then, one or two strands will be used to embroider details. Places with rich colors should be embroidered with threads of different colors several times.

Stitch Guide

1 Apply silk threads of white shades, brown shades, pearlescent aqua shades, and yellow shades to complete the flooded land by means of big free cross stitch. Apply silk threads of white shades, green shades, and brown shades to embroider the small waterfall by means of small free cross stitch.

2 Apply silk threads of black, red, white, brown and yellow shades to complete the hair and the skirt of the standing girl and the part above her waist by means of small free cross stitch. Apply black silk threads and silk threads of brown shades to embroider the hair of the girl washing her hair as well as her skirt and the water jar by means of small free cross stitch. Apply silk threads of white shades to complete the part above her waist by means of big free cross stitch.

3 Apply silk threads of white shades and brown shades to complete the staircase by means of big free cross stitch.

4 Apply silk threads of white shades, green shades, pearlescent aqua shades, and brown shades to complete the hardy banana. Apply the big free cross stitch if veins and blades of leaves are horizontal. Apply small free cross stitch if veins and blades of leaves are vertical.

5 Apply silk threads of brown shades, pearlescent aqua shades, and green shades to embroider palm trees and coconut trees by means of small free cross stitch.

6 Apply silk threads of yellow shades, brown shades, pearlescent aqua shades, and green shades to embroider the crown of other trees by means of hash tag mark free cross stitch.

7 Apply silk threads of brown shades to complete the roof by means of small free cross stitch. Use silk threads of white shades and pearlescent aqua shades to complete the walls of the bamboo pile dwelling by means of small free cross stitch. Apply silk threads of brown shades and pearlescent aqua shades to complete the horizontal log of the bamboo pile dwelling by means of big free cross stitch. Apply silk threads of white shades and pearlescent aqua shades to embroider the sky and the indiscernible trees covered by fog by means of hash tag mark free cross stitch.

婆婆恩濁如大苦海
菩薩安噤得大自在
乃知沸鑊自有清潔
雨華生香雲晬臉月
康熙辛未古揚弟子王心湛書

辛未二月珠山弟子李巖和南敬繪

CHAPTER SIX
SELECTION, COLLECTION, AND PRESERVATION OF EMBROIDERY

Nowadays, along with the increasing expansion and vigor of collection and investment, collection of embroidery is being favored by more and more people. Though there is no overwhelming momentum of other kinds of artworks in the market for the time being, the situation is fairly gratifying and unique. How to satisfy the interest of embroidery collection so as to bring more embroidered artworks into the market? This requires collectors to always bear in mind the coexistence of opportunities and risks of collection and deal with them in a rational attitude. In addition, collectors should also continuously acquire professional knowledge of selecting, collecting, and preserving embroidered articles.

1. Selection and Collection

There has been the collection of exquisite embroidery since ancient times. However, collectors should avoid setbacks due to the lack of professional knowledge and experience, because collection involves knowledge of many aspects such as basic craftsmanship, traditional calligraphy and painting, folk customs, etc. Embroidery lovers should be able to identify features of craftsmanship and art as well as judge whether or not embroidered articles are of high quality, whether or not they are works of noted embroiderers and the extent of their rarity, etc. Only in this way can embroidered articles collected be made worthwhile.

   Meanwhile, lovers should set up a system of collection suitable for themselves before collecting embroidered articles, as well as choose a range for collection. So far, the collection of embroidery is confined to several categories as follows: folk embroidery of daily use, noted embroidery by famous embroiderers along the history, embroidery of imperial court in the Ming and Qing dynasties, religious embroidery, embroidery of Chinese ethnic minorities, and embroidery of drama apparel.

FIG. 50   *Portrait of Avalokitesvara*
Hair Embroidery
Kangxi Period in the Qing Dynasty
Palace Museum, Beijing
Hair embroidery originates from the respect of Buddhist followers to Buddha. Therefore, Buddha is the theme in most cases. Since the hair is marked by considerable tenacity, it is apt to be broken if it is strained too much and the surface of the embroidered article will not be smooth if the hair is not strained enough. So, the embroiderer should be patient enough to incorporate the hair onto the surface desirably. This seems to imply the spiritual cultivation of the embroiderer as an unintended coincidence with the concept of spiritual cultivation before believing in Buddhism.

FIG. 51   Children's shoes by Shao Xiaocheng
Embroidery of daily necessities is associated with every aspect of life, therefore also enjoying excellence and
splendor. These two pairs of children's shoes are featured by ingenious conception since they seek perfection
despite simple craftsmanship with an attractive appearance and durability. People prefer embroidering patterns
of tigers or lions on the children's garments to express their hope that children can be healthy and stay away
from diseases.

With a bright red satin base cloth, the pair on the left is worn in the spring. The tiger ears look smart and
lovely as they are decorated by white down. With a shape of a small lion and the embroidery the same as that for
the tiger head shoes, the pair on the right is worn in the autumn. This pair of shoes is embroidered with shining
sequins. A child wearing such shoes would look very spirited.

Folk Embroidery of Daily Use

As its name implies, such embroidery has an explicit purpose for practical use.
According to the different uses, it can be classified into garment embroidery,
such as pouches, traditional bellybands, shoes (FIG. 51), headbands, sleeve
cuffs, earmuffs, and clothes. Embroidery for furniture decoration includes table
draperies, tablecloths, door curtains, bed curtains, chair covers, pillow covers.
Decorative articles for festivals and celebration were wedding backdrops, hanging
scrolls, plaques, and red veils. In terms of areas, there are such styles of embroidery
as Shaanxi Embroidery (*qin xiu*), Shanxi Embroidery (*jin xiu*), Ethnic Embroidery
of the Qiang (*qiang xiu*), Beijing Embroidery (*jing xiu*), and Kaifeng Embroidery
(*bian xiu*), etc. Embroidery for daily use that deserves to be collected usually
reflects the style of the times and local features. Some embroidered articles for
daily use produced with high quality in recent years also deserve to be collected.

Noted Embroidery by Famous Embroiderers along the History

All kinds of noted embroidery are featured by explicit styles and cannot
be reproduced. Besides, they are mostly circulated in order, in terms of
the embroidery style, seal of the embroiderer, preface and postscript of the
embroidery, and specimen seal impression filed for check-up, etc. Choosing to
collect this kind of embroidery requires more acquisition of related historical
information. Since this kind of works is like the top of the pyramid for

embroidery collection, collector's knowledge reserve regarding Chinese calligraphy and painting is demanded even more. Works of noted embroiderers listed by Zhu Qiqian (1872–1964) in his *Abbreviated Biography of Ancient Female Embroiderers* can be use as reference for collectors (FIG. 52).

Embroidery of Imperial Court in the Ming and Qing Dynasties

Most of the embroidery of this kind is magnificent, simple, and elegant. Though its classification can be roughly referred to that of the folk embroidery of daily use, its craftsmanship is even more fine and exquisite. Garment of the imperial court is one of them. Dragon robes tend to be the first choice for collectors. Dragon robes are featured by strict process of production, and particular regulations. It is especially so with such embroidery collected by the imperial court in the Qing Dynasty. In history, some emperors even directly took part in the design of patterns on the dragon robes. Therefore, there is a very complete collection of dragon robes in the museums, with very few of them scattered in society. As a result, at present, the source of so many embroidered dragon robes in the market is doubtful. Collectors can consult related personnel from the Beijng Palace Museum in which there is the most complete collection of embroidered dragon robes, in order to get to know the truth of embroidered dragon robes collected (FIG. 53).

Religious Embroidery

It includes embroidered religious portraits (such as paintings of Buddhism and Taoism and thangka), embroidered articles for religious ceremony

FIG. 52 *The Rising Sun above Trees with a Long Poem for the Imperial Court*
It is embroidered by Kong Xianpei's wife whose maiden name was Yu, preserved in the Palace Museum, Taipei.

FIG. 53 Embroidered sleeveless jacket

(such as mantra banner flags, canopies, scriptures, Buddha crowns, and *kasaya*) and hair embroidery, etc. There were regulations for most of the embroidered portraits in different historical periods. Embroiderers followed suit, with obvious features of the era concerned. Embroidered articles for religious ceremony are prominently marked by solemnity and seriousness and most of them are free from being gaudy and complex. Particularly in terms of facial expression, fake ones tend to be vulgar, too humanistic, and dispirited.

Hair embroidery is a special kind of religious embroidery. Since the Tang and Song dynasties, there have been more and more followers devoted to Buddhism. As a special variety of embroidery, it uses hair as raw material to embroider the sketch of Buddhist portraits or sketched works associated with Buddhist themes. In contemporary times, hair embroidery is softened like silk through chemical processing of many procedures. Besides, while choosing to bring about hair embroidery in modern times, one had better know that embroiderers should be proficient in handling the evenness and thickness of hair because of its strong toughness. In the course of work, hair can be broken if too much strength is exerted and unevenness would appear if strength is not exerted enough. Therefore, only skilled embroiderers can get rid of defects in handling hair embroidery. While buying it, customers should pay more attention to whether or not sketched lines of hair embroidery are smooth and beautiful. A slight touch at the hair embroidery would enable you to feel the hair stubbles. If hair embroidery feels soft and smooth and the colors look unnatural, it may have gone through chemical processing. So, customers should be careful.

Embroidery of Chinese Ethnic Minorities

Such embroidery is mostly associated with worship for national totems, mythology, legends, and historical stories. Its patterns are exaggerated and deformed, but vigorous. Its craftsmanship is both complex and concise. Embroidered articles used for wedding and festive celebration are more exquisite at any cost. Because many valuable embroidered articles by people of ethnic minorities have been collected by some big museums abroad since the 1970s, most of them seen in the ethnic minorities regions of China are tourist souvenirs of modern times, hence leading to a limited space for collection. Collectors should be cautious in their purchase.

Embroidery of Drama Apparel

It is similar to embroidery of daily use and embroidery of imperial court garment. However, in order to achieve stage effect, embroidery of dramas is more exaggerated and eye-catching in terms of its decoration, while its patterns are simpler and more symbolic, i.e. the so called "costume and paraphernalia" which requires attention when it is taken for collection.

In addition, in the face of rich and colorful embroidered artworks in modern times, it is far-sighted to collect and invest in works of noted embroidery artists in contemporary times in terms of selection and collection. Particular attention should be paid to embroidered articles which have inherited historical cream and further developed artistry. However, with the presence of embroidery in the market, just like calligraphy and paintings in contemporary times, there are also fake works. Some of them also look gorgeous, but they are dispirited because of excessive pursuit of appearance resemblance. Or they may present themselves by means of computer-aided spray painting for copies and patterns and have seals of master embroiderers embroidered.

In order to avoid the possibility of collecting such works, collectors should try to make more contacts with embroidery artists to get to know their attainments and to become familiar with their style of creation. If conditions permit, collectors can also ask to see in person the process of embroidery and take photo or film the process.

Some embroiderers are aware of the loss of the cultural added value of embroidered works. Consequently, they term the behavior of changing embroidery fabrics or threads into a different material as innovation so as to attract people. In fact, there is not actual innovation in the craftsmanship. After getting to know these situations, collectors are able to acquire more rational understanding of collecting embroidery in contemporary times.

2. Appraisal

After having acquired considerable knowledge of embroidered articles, collectors should also learn to identify antiqued, fake, and deceiving embroidery that have inconspicuously appeared due to the popularization and mass enthusiasm of embroidery collection. Therefore, buyers should acquire basic knowledge of counterfeits and be good at observation instead of having blind faith. They should have the spirit of "getting to the bottom" when encountering doubts. Several methods as follows can help readers to make appraisal of embroidery.

Antiqued Embroidery Counterfeited through Color-Smoking and Color-Faking

These are commonly used means for counterfeits among embroidered articles in order to make the surface of newly-produced embroidery appear yellow and old by means of smoking to attract collectors. While finding that their tint is somewhat old, collectors should first make sure if the color of the embroidery front and reverse are consistent. If the tint of the reverse is brighter than that of the front with an obvious smoked smell, it has undoubtedly been counterfeited through smoking (FIG. 54).

To make a piece look old and spotted, people may have two ways to do so.

FIG. 54　Color-smoking and antiqued embroidery

FIG. 55　Color-faking and antiqued embroidery

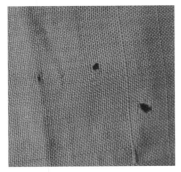

FIG. 56　Non-artificial insect-bite holes

First is colored water from plants that have been soaked for a long time, like tea soup. Second are mixed colors like ochre, indigo, and eosin, etc. After being sprayed or brushed, the colors of embroidered articles appear old and spotted to cheat collectors. Through observation, collectors can find whether or not embroidery threads have completely lost the elasticity of a natural state, whether or not most embroidery threads stick together or become dry and stuck on the fabrics without any trace of movement. These are the most obvious flaws in color-counterfeiting for aged pieces (FIG. 55).

"Old" Embroidery Counterfeited through Insect-Bites

As is known to all, old silk is like rotting rice straw. Real silk articles produced for quite a few years are apt to be bitten by insects and the same is true of embroidered articles. Some people allow insects to bite the embroidery in order to produce the effect of insect-bites on the article and mislead collectors that the embroidery article was made a long time ago.

While finding such embroidered articles with insect-bites, collectors need to take a close look at whether or not the insect-bites are natural (FIG. 56) and whether or not the insect-bites are different from the insect-bites that takes place under natural conditions. For instance, if there are too many insect-bites, almost in an exaggerated way, and these insect-bites are all seen on the fringes of the main composition of the embroidery without affecting its overall appearance, then such insect-bites are likely to be artificially produced. Usually, holes bitten by insects look natural. They can be seen anywhere for insects would not choose to bite at places without embroidery patterns. Moreover, they would not "nibble" at places without any reason.

"New" Embroidered Articles Produced through Old Fabrics

Counterfeiters would first purposefully look for and collect unused old silk fabrics or plain satin damask stored in the elders' homes. Then, they would select corresponding patterns and pictures before inviting professional embroiderers to handle the work. They would stress their requirements and points of attention, by which embroiderers should abide during the process of embroidery, in order to have embroidered articles that conform to its historical appearance. Names of noted embroiderers would be imitated and fake seals of collection would be affixed if embroidered articles of noted embroiderers are falsified. In addition, personnel from professional institutions may be invited to make false announcement that the embroidery conforms to what is recorded in the history books, etc. Such imitated embroidered articles would usually be seen in a fairly big auction, presenting themselves at an astronomical price (FIG. 57).

FIG. 57 An old fabric embroidered with dragon patterns

However, as a common saying goes: "When the evil rises one foot, the virtue rises ten." To have comprehensive knowledge is a way to make judgment of whether embroidered articles are true or false, good or bad.

First of all, collectors should have some knowledge related to the embroidery of past successive dynasties and have a clear idea about needlework and techniques of embroidery in different historical periods, so that they will be able to identify features of corresponding craftsmanship and specify concerned historical periods of the embroidery. Secondly, they should be able to know the basic art features of embroidery, i.e. the school that related embroidery belongs to, because all kinds of embroideries are attached to their respective schools, regional characteristics, and features of the times. Furthermore, collectors should check if fabrics and silk threads of the embroidery are marked by a similar sense of the times concerned and reflect the soul. In addition, collectors should find out if there are original ones collected in the museum, etc. Examination should be conducted from several perspectives. If "new" embroidered articles were truly produced on old fabrics, no matter how authentic they look, flaws would be discovered. If unsure about it, collectors are advised to simply give it up for the time being instead of being in a rush to purchase so as to make sure that the risk is reduced to a minimum.

Cosmetic Embroidery in Contemporary Times

The supreme technique of Chinese embroidery is being replaced by embroidery worked on spray-painted fabrics in contemporary times. This refers to the fact that patterns for embroidery are completed by computer-aided spray-painting on a piece of white cloth before embroidery is done directly on it. It has replaced the traditional craftsmanship of the four noted embroidery schools, with the

FIG. 58 *Peacocks and Peony*
Contemporary
This embroidered article from contemporary times is marked by strong colors and rich patterns. Because of its relatively simple craftsmanship, convenient printing and low cost, the painter does not need to design the painting manuscript or produce a manuscript through hoop, nor does the embroiderer have to know the painting theory very well. Anyone with a little embroidery ability can do it by following the painting. For convenience, it can also be put into the computer in the form of the painting manuscript, which has become very popular in the Chinese embroidery market. Thanks to its outstanding economic return, such application has been imitated by four embroidery schools in China as well as many kinds of local embroidery.

However, since the color quality of inkjet painting of contemporary embroidery is not desirable, the color is apt to fade and the needlework is simplified and assimilated due to the dependence on the original inkjet patterns on the fabrics, the style of embroidery schools in different areas in China is lost completely, having enormously hindered the protection and collection of embroidery, as well as leaving behind hidden problems regarding the copyrights of fine art works.

same manuscript for all sorts of embroidered articles, hence resulting in the loss of previous styles and mediocre craftsmanship. Consequently, the four Chinese embroidery schools are on the verge of extinction. Indeed, it is of immense ordeal with immeasurable risks for collectors to choose valuable embroidered articles from among so many embroidered articles under such a situation (FIG. 58)!

Therefore, in terms of collecting embroidered articles in contemporary times, first, stress should be laid on finding out whether or not embroidered articles are of quite high standards of craftsmanship. Second, collectors should try to find out whether or not there are patterns completed by computer-aided spray-painting on the fabrics so as to avoid early color-fading in the future due to uncontrollable elements. Third, collectors should try to find out whether or not patterns concerned are often seen in the market, so as to avoid buying crafts as souvenirs turned out in mass production. Fourthly, collectors should try to find out whether or not if the style of embroidered articles conforms to the features of noted embroidery schools and if they are of high quality. Only by paying attention to these four points can collectors get contemporary embroidered articles that deserve being collected, with the price insured and the value increased.

3. Cleaning and Preservation

Preservation and storage of embroidered articles are an important link. Improper storage will cause unnecessary economic loss. Though we are not likely to preserve them like those collected in professional museums which are assisted by scientific apparatuses and instruments, common folks also have effective methods for reference.

Removing Dust

When an old embroidered article is bought, such tools should be prepared for use, i.e. a new goat-hair writing brush, a new wolf-hair writing brush, and a rubber air dust blower usually for cleaning camera lenses (FIG. 59). First, use the goat-hair writing brush to slightly brush the surface of the embroidered article. With this done, the floating dust over the surface of the embroidered article is blown by the dust blower for several times. Then, the wolf-hair writing brush is used to carefully brush away dirt and particles that are possibly bigger than dust, or that may conceal themselves in the crevices amidst threads. In particular, there are possibly some residues such as insects that cannot be seen by naked eyes in old embroidered articles. Then, the dust blower is used once more to get rid of floating dust brushed out by the writing brush and writing-brush hair which is likely to have fallen from the brush to ensure the cleanness of the surface of the embroidered article.

FIG. 59   Tools for cleaning embroidered articles

Removing Grease

If grease is found on embroidered articles, never wash it in the water or use soap powder or detergents to do partial washing. It is better to use aviation gasoline. Dip a little gasoline with a cotton tip applicator and gently rub the place with grease which can be easily done away with. Your fingers must be gentle while rubbing it. Don't rush to get rid of the dirt with too much strength in case traces are left on the surface of embroidered articles which cannot be repaired. Distilled water and alcohol can also be tried (FIG. 60).

FIG. 60   Alcohol for getting rid of the dirt

Gentle Wash with Water

Some embroidered garments were possibly worn and used by other people before you bought them. Such kinds of embroidered garments can be washed with water in order to ensure health and safety. However, exceptional care should be taken in order to keep their original shape. First, please get a piece of gauze fabric or a piece of chemical fiber fabric with very dense horizontal and vertical threads

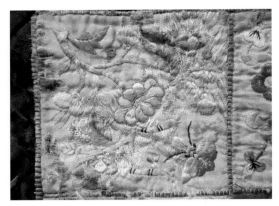

FIG. 61   Gentle washing to protect the gauze cover

FIG. 62   The aging surface of the embroidered article

(FIG. 61) to be sewn to cover the surface of the embroidered article. Put the article into the washing machine. Pour a little hair shampoo. Choose the gentle cycle and the washing process should not be too long. After taking it out of the machine, rinse the article clean in the water. Then, place it flatly between two white towels to squeeze out water. At last, it should be placed flatly to be aired dry and then ironed flat with moderate temperature.

Before washing, check the fiber strength by gently pulling the fiber on the fringe of the embroidered article. If the fiber is broken easily with a gentle pull, it means that the embroidered article is desolated and the fiber is very weak. In this case, washing is not advisable and the status quo can be kept only by way of cleaning (FIG. 62). Furthermore, if the threads break and fall off at many parts of the embroidery article, their original status quo should also be kept as much as possible. Accordingly, washing is not advisable and the status quo can be kept only by the way of cleaning. In a word, washing is not allowed before some of the unwashable elements are ruled out. Action in a rush is not advisable.

Paying Attention to Temperature and Moisture
Usually, embroidered articles should be preserved in room temperature. Never move it from place to place randomly. If they are to be taken from one place to another, the temperatures of both two places should be the same. For example, in China where the north is usually dry and cold while the south is humid and warm, if you want to take embroidered articles from the north to the south, it is better not to do so in the rainy season and misty days in the south, since it would affect embroidered articles to a great extent. On the contrary, if you want to take embroidered articles from the south to the north, you should also find a time when the weather in the south is quite the same as that in the north, such as late autumn in which it is cool with quite appropriate temperature and smaller moisture difference.

In a word, big difference in temperature and moisture is a taboo for

FIG. 63　An embroidered article mounted and inlaid in a picture frame

FIG. 64　Embroidery covered by newspaper and carbon paper for preservation

embroidered articles. It is particularly the case with contemporary embroidered articles whose fabrics were completed by computer-aided spray-painting. The sprayed ink in such kinds of embroidered articles is not stable. Points of attention mentioned above are particularly important if the life of embroidered articles is to be prolonged.

In the Picture-Frame

On the one hand, it serves to offer appreciation at all times and beautify the environment. On the other hand, it is the best way to preserve embroidered articles collected. Embroidered articles in the picture-frame find themselves in a small, quite sealed-off, interference-free, and dust-free environment for a relatively long period of time while getting away from the influence caused by unconscious hand-touch, breath, and the puff of visitors. However, don't hang the picture-frame at a place under direct sunlight for a long time and it would be even worse if embroidered articles are glued in the picture-frame (FIG. 63).

In Other Places

After having been cleaned, embroidery can be directly covered with a layer of translucent white paper when it does not need to be put into the picture-frame for the time being, or does not need to be mounted and hung up. It should be wrapped in the newspaper and placed flatly inside the box, cabinet or desk-drawer in which there should be no chemicals of any kind such as insect repellents and repellent balls. News print ink from the newspaper itself serves as mothproof (FIG. 64). Please don't use moth repellents such as camphor balls since they are harmful to silk woven articles.

There are many ways of collecting embroidery. You can constantly look for them, accumulate, and sum up experience in the course of collecting embroidered artworks.

APPENDICES

Terms of Chinese Embroidery Stitch A to Z

English	Chinese Pinyin	Chinese
appliqué	*tie bu xiu*	贴布绣
battlement filling	*jin wen zhen*	锦纹针
bead work	*ding zhu xiu*	钉珠绣
bead work with back stitch	*ding zhu xiu (ping fu zhen)*	钉珠绣(平伏针)
bead work with couching stitch	*ding zhu xiu (tie xian xiu)*	钉珠绣(贴线绣)
bead work with running stitch	*ding zhu xiu (feng yan zhen)*	钉珠绣(缝衍针)
bead work with stem stitch	*ding zhu xiu (you zhen)*	钉珠绣(游针)
blanket stitch	*suo bian zhen*	锁边针
basic blanket stitch	*ji ben suo bian zhen*	基本锁边针
curved blanket stitch	*qu xian suo bian zhen*	曲线锁边针
flower pattern blanket stitch	*hua xing suo bian zhen*	花形锁边针
long and short blanket stitch	*chang duan suo bian zhen*	长短锁边针
bullion knot	*rao hua xiu*	绕花绣
circle bullion knot	*huan xing rao hua xiu*	环形绕花绣
straight bullion knot	*zhi xing rao hua xiu*	直形绕花绣
chain stitch	*bian zi gu zhen*	辫子股针
ancient chain stitch	*gu bian zi gu zhen*	古辫子股针
closed chain stitch	*bi kou bian zi gu zhen*	闭口辫子股针
open chain stitch	*kai kou bian zi gu zhen*	开口辫子股针
coiling stitch	*la suo zhen*	拉锁针
counted stitch over gauze	*chuo sha xiu*	戳纱绣
horizontal counted stitch over gauze	*heng xiang chuo sha xiu*	横向戳纱绣
slant counted stitch over gauze	*xie xiang chuo sha xiu*	斜向戳纱绣
vertical counted stitch over gauze	*shu xiang chuo sha xiu*	竖向戳纱绣

English	Chinese Pinyin	Chinese
cross stitch	*tiao hua xiu*	挑花绣
basic cross stitch	*ji ben tiao hua xiu*	基本挑花绣
half cross stitch	*ban shi zi tiao hua xiu*	半十字挑花绣
herringbone cross stitch	*chong shi zi tiao hua xiu*	重十字挑花绣
quarter cross stitch	*ping tiao hua xiu*	平挑花绣
encroaching satin stitch	*qiang zhen*	戗针
basic encroaching satin stitch	*zheng qiang zhen*	正戗针
encroaching satin stitch with hidden threads	*fan qiang zhen*	反戗针
interval encroaching satin stitch	*die qiang zhen*	迭戗针
fishbone stitch	*ji mao zhen*	鸡毛针
basic fishbone stitch	*jin mi xing ji mao zhen*	紧密形鸡毛针
open fishbone stitch	*xi shu xing ji mao zhen*	稀疏形鸡毛针
raised fishbone stitch	*jiao cha xing ji mao zhen*	交叉形鸡毛针
free cross stitch	*luan zhen xiu*	乱针绣
big free cross stitch	*da jiao cha zhen*	大交叉针
hash tag mark free cross stitch	*jing zi jiao cha zhen*	井字交叉针
small free cross stitch	*xiao jiao cha zhen*	小交叉针
gold/silver thread couching stitch	*pan jin yin xiu*	盘金银绣
knot stitch	*da zi xiu*	打籽绣
basic knot stitch	*ji ben da zi xiu*	基本打籽绣
knot stitch with a tail	*tuo wei da zi xiu*	拖尾打籽绣
loose knot stitch	*song da zi xiu*	松打籽绣
the Miao ethnicity style knot stitch	*miao da zi xiu*	苗打籽绣
net stitch	*wang wen xiu*	网纹绣
running stitch	*feng yan zhen*	缝衍针
shaded satin stitch	*tao zhen*	套针
long and short shaded satin stitch	*san tao zhen*	散套针
regular shaded satin stitch	*ping tao zhen*	平套针
slanted satin stitch	*chan zhen*	缠针
sparse stitch	*xu zhen*	虚针
horizontal sparse stitch	*heng xiang xu zhen*	横向虚针
vertical sparse stitch	*shu xiang xu zhen*	竖向虚针
split stitch	*jie zhen*	接针
star stitch	*song zhen*	松针
stem stitch	*you zhen*	游针
straight satin stitch	*zhi zhen*	直针
twining thread couching stitch	*chan xian xiu*	缠线绣
weaving stitch	*bian zhi xiu*	编织绣

Bibliography

Editing Committee of Complete Works of Chinese Weaving and Embroidery, comp. *zhongguo cixiu fushi quanji•cixiu juan* [Complete Works of Chinese Embroidered Garments•Embroidery]. Tianjin: Tianjin renmin meishu chubanshe (Tianjin People's Fine-Art Publishing House), 2004

The Palace Museum, comp. *zhixiu shuhua* [Weaving, Embroidery, Calligraphy and Paintings]. Shanghai: Shanghai keji chubanshe (Shanghai Publishing House of Science and Technology for version of simplified Chinese characters), 2005. Hong Kong: shangwu yinshuguan (Commercial Press, Hong Kong Co., Ltd. for version of traditional Chinese characters), 2005.

Chen Juanjuan, *zhongguo zhixiu fushi lunji* [A Collection of Papers on Chinese Weaving and Embroidery]. Beijing: Beijing zijincheng chubanshe (Beijing Forbidden City Press), 2005

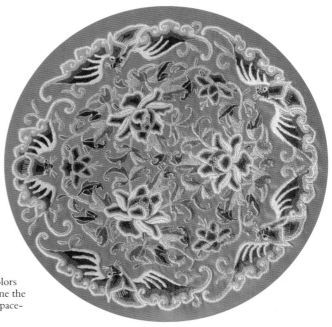

FIG. 65 *Five Happiness to the Family* by Shao Xiaocheng
Knot Stitch in Three Blues
The ring around this article is embroidered with five bats, which stands for "Five Happiness to the Family." In the center, there are interwoven lotus flowers symbolizing more happiness thanks to more children, appearing magnificent with bright red as the base-color. Traditional auspicious patterns coupled with elegant and attractive colors, plus needlework from a long history makes this article the best of its kind.

The three blues refers to three kinds of blue colors in different grades, as the classic color imitating that of blue-and-white porcelain. The main body of the lotus flowers and bats was embroidered by integrating blue colors with knot stitch and gold thread couching stitch to outline the fringes of patterns, thus looking reasonable in terms of space-arrangement and graduation.

Dates of the Chinese Dynasties

Xia Dynasty （夏）	2070–1600 BC
Shang Dynasty （商）	1600–1046 BC
Zhou Dynasty （周）	1046–256 BC
Western Zhou Dynasty （西周）	1046–771 BC
Eastern Zhou Dynasty （东周）	770–256 BC
Spring and Autumn Period （春秋）	770–476 BC
Warring States Period （战国）	475–221 BC
Qin Dynasty （秦）	221–206 BC
Han Dynasty （汉）	206 BC–220 AD
Western Han Dynasty （西汉）	206 BC–25 AD
Eastern Han Dynasty （东汉）	25–220
Three Kingdoms （三国）	220–280
Wei （魏）	220–265
Shu Han （蜀）	221–263
Wu （吴）	222–280
Jin Dynasty （晋）	265–420
Western Jin Dynasty （西晋）	265–316
Eastern Jin Dynasty （东晋）	317–420
Northern and Southern Dynasties （南北朝）	420–589
Southern Dynasties （南朝）	420–589
Liang Dynasty （梁）	502–557
Northern Dynasties （北朝）	439–581
Sui Dynasty （隋）	581–618
Tang Dynasty （唐）	618–907
Five Dynasties and Ten Kingdoms （五代十国）	907–960
Five Dynasties （五代）	907–960
Ten Kingdoms （十国）	902–979
Song Dynasty （宋）	960–1279
Northern Song Dynasty （北宋）	960–1127
Southern Song Dynasty （南宋）	1127–1279
Liao Dynasty （辽）	916–1125
Jin Dynasty （金）	1115–1234
Xixia Dynasty (or Tangut) （西夏）	1038–1227
Yuan Dynasty （元）	1279–1368
Ming Dynasty （明）	1368–1644
Qing Dynasty （清）	1644–1911

Index